DADS TALK
Commu...

THE EMPATHIC FATHER

BY
TORSTEN KLAUS
© 2015

Published by One Tree Family Ltd

ISBN: 978-1-910492-10-9   E-ISBN: 978-1-910492-11-6
First Edition 1

BISAC FAM020000:
FAMILY & RELATIONSHIPS / Parenting /Fatherhood
BISAC SEL040000:
SELF-HELP / Communication & Social Skills

Printed by One Tree Family Ltd throughout the World
http://dadstalkcommunity.org

www.onetreefamily.com

"I think we all have empathy.
We may not have enough courage to display it."

~ Maya Angelou

How often do you feel really understood? Or do you think it's easier at times to count the moments of misunderstanding, frustration, anger, blame and guilt? *The Empathic Father* will shed light on the issues we often experience when we try to communicate with our partner, and when we might get stuck with our daily challenges of parenting.

Fathers of today do want to talk about their feelings, expectations, worries and emotions. They are ready for the next step; A New Generation of Fathers!

We need to encourage every dad to become a part of this new way of authentically communicating with their loved ones to build a compassionate, loving foundation for the future. The more dads who really want to make a change in the way they see their partnerships and parenting, the more we will see happier and balanced families and relationships.

***

"To achieve true equality, we need to start treating fathers as equal parents."

~ Torsten Klaus

Oxford Dictionaries: `empathy′

em|pathy
Pronunciation: /ˈɛmpəθi
Noun

*The ability to understand and share
the feelings of another.*

***

Oxford Dictionaries: `Father′

fa|ther
Pronunciation:/ˈfɑːðə/
Noun

*A man in relation to his child or
children.*

PRAISE FOR THE EMPATHIC FATHER

"This is a book written from the heart of a truly gentle man, we can all learn something from him."

Phil Pryer, Managing Director Lads and Dads Club, UK

"I wish I'd had the opportunity to read this book when I first became a Dad. Torsten reads like a friend, someone who understands what you're thinking and feeling.

Torsten's taken the time to consult some of the best research and advice around. He's selected valuable tips and presented them in a non-judgmental way. By sharing his own experience (and admitting that he doesn't always get it right) you're keen to try some practical ideas for yourself. Some of the suggestions are so simple, you'll be thinking 'why didn't I think of that?'

If you're already on the journey of fatherhood, you'll find this useful as a way of reflecting on your own experience and evaluating your progress. You'll feel encouraged to experiment with a different approach, or look at your situation from a different angle. Above all, you'll understand that you're doing your best and that's what matters!"

Chris Baxter, Broadcast Journalist and Presenter at BBC Radio Gloucestershire

CONTENTS

FOREWORD

My father did a lot for my sister and me. He bought us the latest toys (quite a challenge, growing up and living in former East Germany). He worked long hours and many weekends, even managing to support me financially when I went through rougher times in my life.

I'm thankful for that.

Something was missing though. Something very important: *Emotional closeness and openness*.

We never really *talked*. We never managed to establish a relationship in which we would share our innermost emotions, feelings, aspirations or dreams.

It took me a long time to come to terms with that. And even longer to realise how important it is to talk, to reflect and to open up. Not only for my sake. No, for the sake of my children, my partner and our relationship, friends, colleagues... and somehow, for the sake of society.

Relationships matter. Dads matter.

So why is it so important to have good, honest conversations with your father?

I believe it's about being authentic and empathic. Our journey as humans starts with trusting some very special people - our parents. From our parents we learn through observing and copying. With their guidance, we explore and discover. We try and fail. We try again and may succeed.

I wish I had the chance to talk to my father again. I wish that he had taught me how to be more empathic and gentle when I was a teenager or young man. Maybe with his help I wouldn't have hurt the people in my life that I have.

Many young men need exactly such guidance. Life is so complicated and confusing; for so many years I was craving someone who I could trust, someone who would hold me tight and someone who would emotionally support and challenge me in a respectful way.

THE EMPATHIC FATHER

Many men I talk to have had similar experiences. They lack positive male role models and struggle with 'being the change', which is why I think our society is ripe for, and indeed *needs*, a new generation of men and fathers. To make our families and relationships work we need more understanding and less ego. More empathy and respect; more open dialogue – men being able to have a good talk, sharing honest reflection rather than blame and judgement.

The way we parent our children will ultimately reflect upon our society. If, for example, we either intentionally or inadvertently raise tough and hard boys, we foster a society of tough and hard men. Economy and politics have traditionally been ruled by older, hard, ego-driven or so-called 'strong' men. From behind the safety of their desks they decide right and wrong; these are the men who declare war instead of love.

I sincerely wish for more gentle people to have the power and influence to make big decisions which affect our lives. I call for a society where men, women and transgender live equally... *that includes in our parenting.* As fathers, to raise our children in a gentle way, we need time to spend with them, time to connect deeply, play and share in conversation.

How can this be possible when at the earliest, and probably *most important* time for bonding, fathers in the United Kingdom (UK) are financially forced to return to work after only <u>two weeks</u> of paternity leave (paid at often far less than their standard weekly rate)?

Why do parental discrepancies exist in maternity versus paternity leave allowances in the first place, or force couples to make a trade-off based on salary or gender social expectations? I can't see the new Shared Parental Leave, introduced by the UK-government in April 2015, as a big game changer either. Many families will still face financial pressure. The United States have notoriously even fewer rights, protection and support for parental leave, especially when compared to Scandinavian nations.

Another way is possible.

THE EMPATHIC FATHER

Countries such as Sweden and Germany demonstrate far more progressive attitudes. Swedish parents benefit from a gender-neutral parental leave allowance, which pays 90% of the salary for up to 480 days for the first child. The parents can decide how and when they split their leave and it's no surprise to me that nearly 90% of fathers take paternity leave in Sweden.[1]

Why don't stay-at-home parents get sufficient financial support from their governments? They actually do the most important job in society; *raising the future generation*. Let's not overlook by not accessing state funded care, families bear great personal rather than national economic burden.

Why in this day and age is it still a challenge for mothers to return to employment (even part-time), let alone the difficulties for fathers to arrange more flexible working hours?

---

[1] http://www.economist.com/blogs/economist-explains/2014/07/economist-explains-15

Why are boys still treated by many as the stronger, braver, super-hero, or rougher gender? Because it's been that way for centuries?

Not good enough for me. I want a change.

Let's start here and today. Let's start the gentle talk. Let's embrace our children - girls and boys alike - as something beautiful, special... *human*.

'Human' to me means not being competitive and only interested in my own good, but able to be interdependent with others; to look out for one another, be it in the family, our community or the world. I want my children to grow up as social beings. That means that I need to lead the way in how to be kind to others, how to help those who need it, how to be compassionate and non-judgmental.

This is how I aim to parent my children.

I strive to fulfil their needs for physical and emotional closeness. I love them unconditionally. I don't ask them not to be 'needy' or dependent on me; the more I allow them to be reliant on my wife and I in the early years (having them sleep right beside us parents, carrying them close in a sling, attending to their needs immediately, feeding on demand, allowing them to have their own feelings – be they happy or sad), the more independent they'll become when they are ready for it.

We need a new generation of boys, men, fathers, grandfathers, teachers, politicians, workers, thinkers and dreamers.

Let this be your message:

"You'll lead a successful life, when you don't feel the need to strengthen yourself at the expense of others. When you don't feel the desire to devalue others in order to upgrade your own ego. When you don't need to play a role only to find appreciation. You are a man if you really have something to give."
~ Prof. Dr. Gerald Hüther

So true.

***

This book is not meant to be an instruction manual for parenting or fatherhood (if only such a thing existed!).

In many ways *The Empathic Father* presents some helpful conclusions from my own experience as a father, and from working with many families and their children for more than a decade in various positions such as a Children's Centre Community Family Worker. I also use latest research findings, especially when it comes to child and brain development. But, as you probably know, there is an incredible array of research out there. For every argument or fact you find you'll surely find someone stating the exact opposite.

And that's OK. You are smart enough to come up with your own conclusions; to discern between sources to shape your own opinion, and guide your unique journey into parenting. And that's how it should be.

THE EMPATHIC FATHER

No suggestion herein is offered as a 'should-do' list. I'm not the type of parenting author to tell you what you should or shouldn't try within your own family. Personally, I find it useful to garner some reminders or new ideas as the way forward for me to move on when I find myself stuck, and to improve my skills. Honestly, I have trouble myself to adhere to all these suggestions, and often enough I realise how hard it is to change ingrained behaviour, to keep calm in a crisis, and to indeed be truly empathic.

I have tried very hard to keep my chapters and writing short. I know how important time is to all of us nowadays. Especially to people like you and me: parents. So, enjoy reading this book and take from it whatever you like. It's your very personal journey of parenting and fatherhood. This is what I'm finding works for my family, so quite possibly it could help yours too.

Make it so.

***

Thank you…

...for reading this book! Yes, I mean it: we need every single father for this project. Because the more dads who really want to make a change in the way they see their partnerships and parenting, the more we will see happier and balanced families and relationships.

Your kids will thank you. Agreed, that could take some years, but it will happen – especially as they themselves find out what it is like to parent empathically.

We can do this. Together.

***

SO. WHAT'S ALL THIS FUSS ABOUT EMPATHY THEN?

In this book I'll shed light on the issues we often experience when we communicate, and when we inevitably get stuck in our daily challenges of parenting.

How often do you feel really *understood* by your partner or children? Or do you think it's easier to count the moments of misunderstandings, frustrations, anger, blame and guilt? Yep, many of us will more readily identify with the latter.

Let's start from the beginning. Why do we need empathy, or could we just do without?

Did you know that about fifty percent[2] of new parents face a sharp change in their relationship and communication in the first year after the birth of their baby? *Fifty percent* - that's every second couple. So, it could be you or your friends. But it's likely to be at least one of you.

Quite shocking, eh?

There is that loving, gentle, understanding couple who have spent a great deal of time together, and then one of their biggest wishes and desires - a baby - comes along, and everything seems to break down. Suddenly these two lovers start to argue, feel disappointed and frustrated... and blame each other. Therefore, learning to be more

---

[2]https://www.nct.org.uk/sites/default/files/related_documents/OPOPromotinge motionalhealthinthetransitiontoparenthood.pdf

empathic will help you in your partnership as well as in your parenting.

To get this right we need to step back, watch and observe, do some active listening without judging, and – of course – we need a big, warm infusion of empathy.

Yes. We'll be alright,
but we have to work on this. Together.

WHEN YOU'RE NOT ALWAYS AROUND: SINGLE PARENTING OR PART-TIME PAPA

I've written this book mainly from the first-person-perspective. Many ideas, suggestions and reflections are based on what I myself have observed, experienced or read. When I had nearly finished my book, my friend Moira kindly read it. She gave me awesome feedback and inspired me to make changes and amendments.

She also asked me some very good questions, one of which was, *"What about the single dads? And the dads who are less around. Fathers who for whatever reason live separated from their children. Is your book for them too?"*

Gosh, I felt a lump in my throat. Of course, life is far more complex. The way I live doesn't apply to everyone else.

There are around two million single parents in the UK[3]; that's a quarter of all families with children. It is also estimated that one in three children in the UK will experience parental separation before the age of sixteen. And I could give your more numbers. Numbers you would forget in an instant; but behind numbers we find stories. Real stories about real people; our kids, their parents... *families.*

Yes, people make many decisions in life. They fall in love. They have a child. They feel their relationship doesn't work. They separate. They fall in love again... Or sometimes love turns into anger

---

[3] http://www.gingerbread.org.uk/content/365/Statistics

and hatred. Couples once inseparable start to blame each other. They may get verbally aggressive, or even physically. They might go to court and one parent (yes, it's often the father) voluntarily or otherwise, leaves the family home.

Sometimes people have little control over what happens to them in their lives. Illness and death can tragically strike out of the blue. Suddenly, an intact family can be destroyed by the hammer of fate, leaving a single parent behind.

There are millions of other possible scenarios out there. However, the one thing I want to focus on for now is *the children*.

Whatever decisions we make in our lives, we need to put our children into the centre of everything. Life can be mean, it can hurt, and it can often feel unfair. You name it. But above all these difficulties one parent might experience, we should never forget to observe our children's needs, dreams and wishes.

THE EMPATHIC FATHER

Whether you're a full-time single dad or you see your kids less than you ideally would like... even if you are not a biological father, but have merged into a ready-made step-family... if you consider yourself in whatever way to be a parent, a *father,* I've written this book for you.

I have met many fathers who have been through nasty divorces, fathers who had to fight for their right to see their children, fathers who split up with their partner on friendly terms, and those whose work situation doesn't allow them to be around their family as much as everyone would wish for.

They all have their story. They all have my sympathy. And they all have my deepest respect. Because most dads I have met have always tried to be there for their children, regardless of the circumstances.

So, I wish for you to take from my suggestions and tips what feels right to you and what fits into your personal life circumstances. It might help you make changes, where you feel they are necessary, or confirm how you are feeling, or just raise questions you may want to answer.

In the third part of this book I talk about relationships between fathers and their partners. Yes, I know if you have decided to part ways with the mother of your children you probably are not aiming for a physically intimate relationship with your ex. Fair enough. But you might need to communicate with them. And you might want to leave behind some of the blame-and-shame-attitude. Yes? No? Well, it's up to you. And this part might also be of importance should you start another relationship – even if that brings a whole host of issues that I have not touched on in this book (but hey, there is always a next book, and I would welcome your thoughts on what you would like to read about).

THE EMPATHIC FATHER

Whatever you decide, take from this book what feels important to you. Be around your kids as much as you are able. Your children might see that relationships change, but they also should see that you care as best as you can in the circumstances that your family finds themselves in. Make loving them your priority — that also means respecting who they love and feel close to, even if that feels hard.

Choose to be the best kind of father that you can be.

Choose empathy.

Choose love.

PART ONE: YOU &
SOMETHING NEW

1. THE JOURNEY BEGINS

*"One of the greatest gifts parents can give
their child is a happy relationship between
Mom and Dad, a partnership in which the ideas
and feelings of both parents are equally
considered and included."*
~ Meryn Callander

This is such an exciting time. Don't worry; I won't give you a checklist to see whether or not you're prepared for the birth. There are plenty of suggestions out there - search for such lists if you feel that you need them.

It might be only a few weeks or days to go until you will enter a completely new stage of your life as you await the birth of your baby. Yes, you have probably heard it so often already; *nothing in your life will be as before.*

That's true. Fatherhood will change everything.

I wish you enough time for you and your partner to get prepared. I don't mean buying stuff (you actually will be surprised how little you'll need, especially for the first couple of years); I'm talking about you as a person, a man, a partner, a father-to-be.

Right now I will not talk about all the beautiful things a life with a new baby will bring. I'm sure you'll discover all that yourself. I'm convinced you'll give and do your very best to be a loving father.

***

I remember being very excited during my wife Nedua's first pregnancy. I couldn't wait for the due date to come nearer. I also felt a little nervous and unsure, but hey, I read parenting and relationship books, as partners we did talk a lot... so I thought we would be fine.

THE EMPATHIC FATHER

Yes, my wife and I were fine... *ish*.

Truth was, despite our dreams the first eighteen months with our baby were an emotional roller coaster.

I had moments where I felt very low. Nedua and I argued a lot. I tried to help wherever I could but no effort seemed good enough to her... and when it came to the baby, I felt she was constantly checking whether I did things right or not (obviously I didn't do them to her satisfaction, in *her way*). At the same time I was aware that Nedua felt depressed, isolated and often exhausted.

We worried a lot, but didn't talk much.

Such low feelings can have various reasons: birth trauma, health problems, being isolated, sleep deprivation, a changed self-image and altered sense of purpose in the world etc.

But it's not only women who can experience the 'baby blues' post-natally...

... What really struck me was that I found out new fathers can feel low too.

This can have various reasons. Many new fathers feel that even though their life has been turned upside down they are expected to (or indeed, expect themselves to) just continue as before; go out to work, entertain an active social life, continue with their hobbies...put simply, to be just like before baby came along.

In reality, our emotional life, our relationship and home is in chaos. It takes time to adjust, and mostly we need to work on it becoming more settled. We as men are often 'fixers', we want to be able to control and conclude situations. Whether it's a colicky night, or a tempestuous, capricious toddler; a baby is sent to remind us that life is never that simple.

Becoming a father also triggers memories from our own childhoods. Seeing our partner attend to our baby can sometimes be a very emotional experience in terms of seeing what we might not have received ourselves as young children. Babies are born completely helpless and unable to survive on their own. They need at least one attachment figure, who will always be there to care for them. More than anything else, even food and drink, babies need love and care to know that they are not alone – and therefore can survive.

That means babies need someone who is continuously responsive to their needs. Only once they internalise that they can trust their caregivers, and go into the world, securely attached – knowing that they are loved unconditionally, will they have an inbuilt trust in the world around them. This is the Theory of Attachment (developed by John Bowlby[4]) in a nutshell. How our own attachment needs were met by our caregivers reflects the needs and fears we now have as adults.

When I was only about two months old my parents went on a two-week-holiday and left me

---

[4] http://www.simplypsychology.org/bowlby.html

with a neighbour. I can only imagine how much I must have cried and screamed being cared for by a stranger. From very early on my ability to trust and love people was damaged. More disappointments later on shaped the way I would form relationships and choose partners as an adult.

I was looking for relationships where I felt safe, unconditionally loved, and appreciated for who I am. But still, I couldn't really *trust*. Fears of being dumped by my partner made me end relationships first. I didn't know it but I was looking for that loving mother-care that I had missed as a baby and small child. In Nedua, my wife, I eventually found that person. She gave me that instant feeling of security and filled my empty glass with love, respect and empathy.

***

But what happened after the birth? All the attention I was used to receiving from her suddenly went to the baby. She had only eyes for him; all her previously unconditional love and nurturing seemed to be unceremoniously withdrawn from me.

So where and how could I meet *my* attachment needs? You might think 'what a selfish guy... of course the baby is the centre of life, isn't it?'

Indeed, all our parental love, attention and nurture went to him: 24/7. But we are human beings who need nurturing too. Slowly and step by step, Nedua and I learned that together. By looking at our own attachment fears and needs, we could start exploring which situations and emotions were most intensely triggering our reactions. Our starting point was to talk. Reflection, empathy, crying, hugging, holding and talking were our tools to start the healing process.

Our children are six and three years old now. With our second child we didn't experience such low moods. With more confidence and experience we solved problems before they got too big. And yes, we're still working on *Us*; on our non-violent communication and the way we deal with the emotional wounds from past and present. On our marriage and capability as connected partners and parents.

So why am I writing all this gloomy stuff? To get you ready and prepared for fatherhood. You can buy the coolest buggy, the softest baby duvet, the most colourful sling and the flashiest organic cloth nappies in the whole world, but that won't help you in dealing with your emotions, worries and expectations.

To be a loving and caring father yourself, your glass of emotional confidence and security should be rather full, even if at times it feels like it is spilling.

LOOK BACKWARDS BEFORE GOING FORWARDS

Look at your own childhood, and your previous romantic relationships for that matter. The impact our fears and need for security have on the present moment can be immense.

Start talking – the earlier the better – to your partner (and/or other people close to you who know you best, and who impact on your parenting) and explore your past: go back to your childhood and see what actually happened there.

Try and be honest rather than gloss over things. It can be difficult to be critical when it comes to honestly examining the decisions that our parents made historically. It might mean that a rose-tinted image of your 'perfect childhood' tarnishes somewhat, which can be hard at first.

It's important to look at your parents and their choices with the empathy you are seeking for your future relationship success, rather than seeking to attach blame or negative judgement. In some cases you will simply not be able to understand why they did things the way they did, and for your own peace of mind you should learn to accept that. In others, you will be able to see they were doing the best they could with the knowledge and resources available to them at the time, just as you are trying to do now. As your own children in time will also come to realise.

Forgive them and yourself, in order to move forwards for the relationships you want to experience, rather than lamenting what has passed. Awareness of the impact of such experiences is the first step in identifying your current needs, and reasons why you may react positively or negatively to particular challenges you will find yourself facing as a new parent.

PREPARE YOUR RELATIONSHIP FOR THE TRANSITION TO PARENTHOOD

Look at your current conflicts in your life and in your partnership. Ask yourself questions like: *"What makes me angry? What do I do when I get angry?"*

Are you able to see the emotions underneath that anger? Often they are linked to our attachment needs and fears. These could be sadness, fear of abandonment, or the need to feel safe and loved. If you learn how to communicate these emotions clearly, your partner's reactions will be very different than at times of getting angry (I explore this in more depth in Part Three of this book).

Indeed the matter you are fighting about suddenly seems irrelevant — as what you probably really want to say is, *"I am afraid, please hold me,"* or "I feel helpless and unsure of what to do, *do you still love me/care for me?"*

Reflect, think, cry, laugh, let it out, be vulnerable. The emotional preparation that you allow yourself to do prior to the upheaval of the arrival of a new and demanding little person into your relationship will better allow you to weather the more challenging moments that are inevitably to arrive.

The best thing you can give to your child is experiencing and modelling your ability to form close connections with your partner and others; it will make you a gentler parent and your kids will hugely benefit by seeing you work through life's ups and downs together.

That's where your journey starts in becoming an authentic father.

Have a positive birth experience and enjoy the days and weeks when walking into the land of parenthood.

2. BIRTH AS A BEAUTIFUL EVENT

You know what I find quite disgusting and upsetting? The way births are predominately presented in media.

Especially in those Hollywood movies where the mother-to-be is uncomfortably positioned on her back in a hospital bed, screaming her head off while a nurse shouts at her to PUSH NOW. Meanwhile, the father-to-be paces the corridor up and down for the hundredth time... smoking, looking nervous and insecure like an animal on the run. But then, just in time, a very nice, relaxed, white middle-class gentleman in doctor's dress appears and expertly brings everything under control. A few minutes later he announces: *"Congratulations, it's a boy."* Now the brand new

41

father faints, and mum cries as baby is wheeled off to the nursery.

Cue happy ending.

F**k Hollywood; real life is very different. Birth can indeed be clinical, detached and scary if we let it be, yet it can also be powerful, empowering and beautiful when we trust and yield to the process of nature.

I truly believe parents-to-be should get supported in the choices they make. About where the birth of their baby is going to take place, and how they want midwives or other helpers and professionals to respond and support.

I believe that everyone should have the right to a natural or unassisted birth should they want one (where medical intervention is the exception rather than the norm), in the case of healthy pregnancy and delivery. Birth is a right of self-determination, the *ultimate human act* if you will. To be swept, harassed or scared into a birthing situation that feels unnatural to you as a couple is to fundamentally alter one of the most profound experiences of the human condition. Own your birth, and have the confidence in your ability to have a beautiful experience, irrespective of the degree of intervention requested or required.

I don't know how you feel about birth preparations, but I certainly found it helpful to listen to other birth stories. The good ones. Yes, things can go wrong and it's vital to have a plan B as back up. But I believe focusing on the positive will also create a more relaxed and confident atmosphere... because hey, that is exactly what your partner is going to need.

Your emotions and inner state during your partner's labour will undoubtedly affect that of your partner, and indeed her confidence, calmness and success in labour. If you are panicking, she will pick this up at a time she most needs your strength and belief in her body to birth your baby smoothly into the world.

During labour and birth you need to be your partner's and your baby's advocate, because it might not be that she is effectively able to speak for herself in that vulnerable situation. The more you know about birth (see some suggested reading in the index) and local hospital, maternity-led unit, or homebirth protocol, then the better you can prepare yourself.

Sit with your partner to write and agree a birth plan stating exactly what you want (and don't want) for the birth of your baby. You as a couple know what's best for your baby, and your family.

If there does happen to be a medical emergency, medical staff ask very few questions of you when needing to act quickly. Should you find yourself in such a situation, where you are asked what to do next, it helps to simply ask the staff, *"is xyz going to risk the life of my baby, or partner?"* If the answer is yes, you don't need to think twice about what to do next. If no, you have a chance to reconsider your options; to consider what your partner would best prefer, to wait a little longer before taking a particular course of action, to try changing positions, getting in/out of water, having a snack etc. Labours have a way of working themselves out in many circumstances; you may find the baby makes the decision for you if you trust in your partner's body to know what it needs.

We planned home births with both of our children. Before the first, Nedua and I had to deal with some comments from my sister as she regarded home birth to be unsafe. Well, we had a lovely birth, with our eldest son being born on the sofa. Awesome. But even more touching was the birth of our second son. I believe the moment he came to us was one of the greatest moments in my life. That's probably what most parents say. Let it be.

Here and now I would like to share the moments of the day my youngest son, Marlo, was born. Nedua and I have both written our birth stories to capture such a special day in our lives.

***

MARLO'S EARTHSIDE JOURNEY

06.40: Just after we wake, Nedua's waters break.

Morning: Our day starts as normal. We have breakfast and do the morning routine. Later on I take our eldest to the local shops where we meet our adopted Granny, as we had agreed beforehand. She then takes him on a little shopping trip, they go to the museum and the park for ice cream and finally some fun on the playground.

Back at home, Nedua and I relax together by looking at photographs from our son's recent birthday party. Soon after, we both listen to a natal hypnotherapy CD (which Nedua had used throughout pregnancy), we have pizza for lunch and again, take time to chill out. I start massaging Nedua's belly with birthing oil. She gets the first light contractions.

13.30: We decide to go for a walk. On the way we enjoy an ice cream and we also buy cake. Nedua's contractions get stronger and she needs to stop and rest in between. She places her arms onto my shoulders and takes deep breaths.

14.30: Coffee and cake at home (yes, we're German)

Afternoon: The contractions get stronger and more regular. Nedua stays calm and focuses on deep long breaths.

16.50: I pick up our son from Granny's house. Nedua is upstairs in the bedroom. She leans on the bed posts, looks out of the window and breathes with the contractions. I promise to be quick; I want to be with her, every moment.

17.30: My son and I sit at the table and eat dinner. My wife sits next to us on one of those pregnancy balls (yes, the big gym ones) and focuses on breathing and the contractions. After dinner I take my son upstairs for the evening routine (brushing teeth, good-night-story, talking about the day, lights off), which I try to do in double speed. I hear my wife from downstairs. Yes, the contractions are strong by now. I hope my son goes to sleep very quickly.

18.30: My son is asleep and I go downstairs. Nedua sits in the bath tub. The contractions are very strong now —mirroring the strength I can see in my wife. I go back into the lounge to inflate our birthing pool, which takes only three or four minutes. Back in the bathroom I massage her back and breathe with her. Next I want to attach the hosepipe onto the tap to fill up the pool. I had tried this before; on that previous occasion it had worked; now it didn't. After a few trials I give up — slightly stressed and annoyed. Nedua says she needs me now. Everything goes quickly from there.

19.00: Nedua asks me to call the midwife. I do the phone call and the midwife promises to be with us in the next ten minutes.

Between 19.05 and 19.10(?): Nedua says she can feel the baby's head. I can't see it but already with the next contraction the baby is born. She holds him. I'm surprised but also very touched at the same time. She holds our baby and I gently loosen the cord from his neck. We look at our baby and everything seems to be so still, so quiet and peaceful. Our boy is calm and relaxed. He cuddles onto my wife's skin and slowly arrives in this world.

A perfect moment. I bathe in happiness.

Shortly after 19.10: The midwife arrives. She looks at me. She looks at Nedua. She looks at the baby. Then she smiles and says *"Well done."*

Around 19.30: Nedua and our baby are still in the bath. The placenta arrives. I give some homeopathic medicine to her to relieve any discomfort.

Evening: Nedua, the baby and I sit on our sofa. We enjoy this special time for the three of us. The midwife kindly cleans the bath tub and does her paperwork in the kitchen. We don't let our son be measured or weighed tonight. That can wait until tomorrow.

At this very moment we just want to hold him and watch him. What a joy! At nine o'clock the midwife leaves us for the night. I wash the placenta, which is still attached to the cord and baby's navel (check out lotus birth if you like), then we go upstairs to sleep. Our eldest is fast asleep and we join him in our family bed. The night stays quiet and we sleep astonishingly well.

Just before I go to sleep I have that one thought in my mind: Now I'm a father of two children.

With a big smile I go to sleep as well.

***

I wish for you to have such a beautiful, nurturing and positive experience. Birth is hardly ever as they say in the movies. That doesn't mean your birth has to look exactly the same. No, not at all. Make it your very special event.

3. AFTER THE BABYMOON...
WHEN THINGS CHANGE

Birth can be so beautiful. The birth of my eldest son took place at home as well, but he decided to start life on the sofa. As I've said, babies often have their own ways of letting us know how they wish to come into the world.

How was it for you? What was your birth story? Did things go as planned? Was it what you/your partner had expected or hoped for? Reflecting on this experience is powerful for fathers too.

***

So, baby is here. Congratulations!

Let's go back to the time after my first son was born... before I really had a clue what I was supposed to be doing.

As I have previously divulged, I was so excited about becoming a father. I felt well prepared and couldn't wait for the baby to be here. During my paternity leave I felt as protected as if I were in a cosy nest. Walking on air, some might say.

However, things changed quite a bit when I returned to work.

I did my best to support Nedua as a new mother. From work I would rush home to find her exhausted, the baby crying and general chaos. It is hard to imagine what a day in the life of a new mum looks like. Indeed some fathers might wonder *'why isn't she actually managing to look after our baby and the household, seeing that she has so much time...'*

I came across an article somewhere saying that you, as a father, should always assume that your partner's day at home with baby was harder/more stressful than your own at work. This in a way opened my eyes a little, and I only came to understand much later what it was like to look after my children and keep on top of household chores. I came to expect nothing, to accept the situation *as it was* and tell myself that this was a tough time of our lives, but one that would pass.

Normally I would either be with our baby or start the washing up, in order to have at least two clean plates in the house. Still, I struggled with getting comments or gazes from my equally tired wife. My initial high turned into feeling low and the bitter taste of rejection lingered silently inside.

I started asking questions of myself such as:

Does she still love me?

Am I a good enough father?

No-one had prepared me for these emotions. I felt my life turned upside down and in the outside world I was expected to just return to normal, leaving me no time or space to reflect or simply breathe and find my feet.

While women find this time equally hard, support is comparatively easier to access. Before and after the birth of our son everyone seemed so supportive towards my partner: the midwife, the health visitor, family and friends. While Nedua was able (*expected*, even) to share her new experience with other mums at various baby groups, being nurtured and heard, I shut down emotionally and sometimes even physically (by becoming unwell).

So, let's check this out: I didn't know what was happening to me and had no idea that many fathers experience similar emotions and for some it turns into Postnatal Depression (PND).

Yes, three to ten percent of fathers[5] (with even higher numbers reported in the USA) can suffer from PND. Up until now there has been very little research or general knowledge about it as men 'don't do' the post birth check-ups with

---

[5] See References

professionals, where maternal PND is often recognised; the Health Visiting team are designed with the health of baby and mother in mind. Dads can be left feeling like a by-product of the process.

So, what are the signs and symptoms of postnatal depression in men (which by the way can begin almost immediately, or a few weeks to months after, your baby's birth)?

- Tiredness, headaches and generalised pain
- Irritability, anxiety and anger
- Loss of libido
- Changes in appetite
- Feelings of being overwhelmed, out of control and unable to cope
- Engaging in risk taking behaviour
- Feelings of isolation and disconnection from partner, friends or family
- Withdrawal from intimate relationships and from family, friends and community life
- Increased hours of work as a part of the withdrawal from family etc.
- Increased use of drugs or alcohol instead of seeking treatment for depression

Generally, it is believed that when their partner suffers from PND, men are more affected; while this is certainly a contributing factor, this isn't always the case. Men can and do experience this independently, and in their own right, rather than only as a by-product of their partner's experience.

SO WHY IS PND IN MEN MORE COMMON THAN WE THINK?

There are several factors contributing to PND; a history of depression or anxiety, lack of emotional and social support, a traumatic birth experience, difficulty adapting to the change in family and relationship dynamics, financial worries, unmet expectations, insecurity around sex and sleep problems. So many factors.

However, after much research I also believe that many men have not yet recognised and reflected upon their own childhood and the resulting needs and fears, which especially when becoming a father, are a big contributing factor to inner balance and whether we are able to have a strong, nurturing relationship.

It is believed that when becoming a parent many memories of our own birth and childhood are stirred up. What has been a seemingly unimportant part of our adult life suddenly comes into the fore front.

Why is that?

Firstly, many men struggle with their new identity and role of being a father, and especially so when they have no role model for guidance. If we don't grow up watching other close men raising their children, how are we supposed to know what's right or wrong? I didn't feel addressed by much of the parenting literature out there, and certainly not inspired by my own father's child raising skills. I'm sure I'm not alone in this experience; it's something which many of you may relate to.

Secondly, watching our partner showering our baby with love and lots of physical contact can trigger feelings of jealousy, because for one we might not have experienced this kind of closeness with our own mother, and secondly because we now need to share our partner physically and emotionally.

That's what happened after the birth of my son: all the attention I had been receiving and craved from Nedua as my wife went suddenly to the baby as his mother.

So where and how could I meet my needs for love and physical contact? We started to argue and blame each other for what we saw as the failure of our relationship.

**

I came across the brilliant work of Meryn Callander, who wrote the book *Why Dads Leave: Insights and Resources for When Partners Become Parents.*

She says: *"Ironically, the better the mother is able to nurture her child, the more likely the father will be to re-experience his childhood wounding because he sees even more of what he didn't get."*

Many men feel guilty or even ashamed of these feelings, some resentful or angry at their partner or child. A lot of new fathers find themselves alone with these feelings. Helpless and unable to share with anyone, they retreat emotionally as the pain of emotional isolation is so hard to bear. As a result of this, some men also decide to leave the family.

Great, so all gloomy and hopeless then? Not at all. You can change it around if you think you might head into the direction of developing a depression, or harbouring such negative feelings.

My mantra here is: *Start talking* – the earlier the better – to your partner and explore your past. Explore your childhood and look at what actually happened before coming back to your current conflicts. See how you respond in arguments, check how you feel. If you learn how to recognise and communicate these emotions clearly, to show your vulnerability and open up, you can start healing past wounds and establish a strong relationship culture in which you connect deeply rather than get lost in the cycle of arguments, resentments and withdrawal.

Here are three bullet points to summarise how you can approach the tougher times of change:

One: The opposing demands of work and family can feel stressful, as there isn't enough time for either and you end up being tired and exhausted. It is important for you as a father to take some time to recharge too. Once your child is in bed can you go out, perhaps once a week, do something you love? Don't feel guilty doing it, your partner needs you fully recharged. Once your batteries are full, offer the same opportunities to your partner: Take the baby while she's having a hot bath or organise a nice afternoon for her and some friends, while you're in charge of baby/the housework/dinner for the evening.

TWO: Spend as much time as you can with the baby and don't be offended by your partner if she suggests you do things differently (she might be totally right, and then you'll find out for yourself anyway. Or you invent *your* way, one which she has not tried yet. That's fine and could work equally well - just give it a try). The more you do it, the more confident you will get.

THREE: Don't ever underestimate the importance of you being around. Especially in the early days it can seem like you are not 'needed'. You are. Every time you interact with your baby you are building a bond. Every time you support your partner you are strengthening the family bond and therefore building your child's safe 'nest.'

The transition from a life as a couple to life as a family is a huge one. Every transition happens over a stretch of time; it requires a lot of patience, communicating positively, adapting to new roles and especially loving kindness and extending forgiveness towards yourself and understanding towards your partner.

You will make mistakes, and yes, that's ok. It's important to open up, get help, connect with other new fathers, find local support services, talk to your doctor, or perhaps start a Dads' group. Use every opportunity to bond with your child (they need you to), make time to re-connect to your partner every day. Be authentic and honest. And reap the rewards of communication.

HOW TO BOND WITH YOUR BABY

Many men feel obsolete when first becoming a father. We, who can't breastfeed, who perhaps don't have the patience or knack to sooth a colicky evening cry? We, who might worry about our hands handling such fragile tiny bodies, who don't understand how the poppers and nappies work, and which end to deal with first in an emergency situation?

What can we as fathers do to foster a strong bond from the first moment on in our child's life?

▪   Cuddle your baby skin to skin as often as possible – yes *you* can soothe them too! Some dads in fact find they are the ones who have the magic touch when needed, or mama is feeling 'touched out' and needs to go to the bathroom in peace.

■ Go for walks with your baby in a sling so they get to know you and your smell. They will even recognise your voice from the time in the womb, so tell baby stories or simply talk about what you see around you (this can even become a mindfulness practice in noticing details and sensation around you).

■ Take baths with your baby. Have baby lie on your tummy and relax together.

■ Sing some songs or rhymes. You can make them up if you can't remember any, or choose your favourite hits – who says babies just like lullabies?

■ When it's time for a nap, cuddle up to your baby. Have her lie on your tummy (possibly after she has been fed), but make sure if you are both going to fall asleep, that you do so safely. Recommendations are to never sleep with your baby on a sofa, or anywhere that they can accidentally become trapped in soft furnishings. It is perfectly possible to sleep safely with your baby, as long as sensible precautions and common sense are exercised. See suggested references at the back of the book.

■   While your partner is feeding your baby, why not just sit with her? Perhaps read her a story, talk to her, make her a drink, give her a massage, or cook some food for the evening meal or the next day. Ask her what would make things easier for her/what would she need to feel good right now?

There is so much you can do. Dads are definitely very much in need, even in those early days when all baby seems to do is eat and sleep. Is there a particular task you can 'take ownership' of, something unique to you and your child... you may even find that you are the one that manages to change nappies with one hand behind your back whilst maintaining that smile on little one's face.

Priceless.

4. SLEEP DEPRIVED FATHERS AREN'T HAVING SEX. RIGHT?

Once the baby has arrived, many new parents would confess that their sex life basically came to a full stop. I think some of us accept the fact that it's just a phase and are happy with having sex reside at the bottom of their priority list. However, others are not as content with how their love life is developing but are unsure or simply too drained to do something about it. After all, what can you do when you're both too tired, feeling unconnected and up all night?

I believe intimacy after giving birth can be a great healing force, and I would encourage women and men not to abandon being a lover when becoming a parent.[6]

---

[6] www.parentsaslovers.com

It is important to give yourselves time, and to not confuse a lot of sex with a great relationship. Sex does not mean love and vice versa.

It is difficult sometimes not to despair; especially when you and your partner have different views about your desired level of intimacy. I would like to stress the importance of a close connection, loving communication and tenderness, which are all available to you without having penetrative sex. And for many they actually are a pre-requisite for having a fulfilling physical relationship.

As I see it the problem lies deep within society. Our culture is obsessed with a certain type of sex (exacerbated with porn images, that some individuals find very difficult to rid themselves of), which can feel more like a burden than a turn-on to new parents.

Wherever we go we are saturated with all manner of images of naked, half-naked and photoshopped women. Whether it's getting a paper from the local shop, where over-dimensional breasts on magazines are prominently displayed, or it's waiting for a bus, which arrives covered in big adverts for a dating agency. Or when we quickly scan the online news and — again, so-called sexy images invite us to click them for the ultimate adventure.

All these images and ads transport one message: Sex. And even more important, that *woman want sex* - anytime and anywhere. Always ready for their man, just waiting for his call or his click.

Really? With this absurd message in mind, men wonder: *Is my partner normal?* Why isn't she doing an erotic dance performance to get me into bed? Where is her lust and passion for hot and wild nights? Why is everyone else but *me* getting physical?

When speaking to other men (and especially, fathers), I was surprised how many confirm that exact picture of the so-called *'cold bed'* and frustrating attempts of failing to have sex. Sometimes these disappointments and frustrations end up in watching porn or looking outside of the marriage for a lover. Or even it's us that are the ones that aren't especially in the mood, even though the message is that we should be ever-ready for any opportunity; we are just as exhausted as our partners.

So here we are: no sex + high frustrations = unwanted tensions and stress. Yes, some men or women consider looking elsewhere. That might help in the short run but often will have a disturbing or (more likely) destructive impact on trust in the relationship.

It is important to look at what it is that you actually need. Often this is not sex, but appreciation, love and acceptance. When you are aware of that and share your emotions with your partner, she/he is likely to be more welcoming and open to intimacy, and maybe new ways of having sex than when feeling pushed or faced with a frustrated lover.

LET ME INTRODUCE YOU TO TANTRA:

I believe that Tantra, especially for exhausted and tired parents, is an excellent way to enjoy intimacy again without the pressure that many parents feel when it comes to making love.

Tantra originates in India. It means 'woven together' or 'connecting with inner self.'

I felt drawn to this practice that has relaxation as a central theme. It involves practices like deep and conscious breathing. A tantric approach is about slowing down, focusing on the here and now rather than being overtly goal-orientated.

One of the first practices you might try for example is 'soul gazing.' You find a comfortable space, when all is quiet in the house, and sit face to face with your partner, looking into each other's eyes. It is such a simple yet beautiful way to connect with another person.

From here, once you initiate that deep connection, it is so much easier to feel what the other likes. You might want to caress your partner and see where it takes you.

Tantric sex is also used as a form of sexual healing. It can release emotional wounds from past traumatic experiences that are stored in the muscle tissue of the body, and which manifest themselves as different symptoms; some are vaginal pain during intercourse, inability to orgasm, premature ejaculation, vaginal dryness, and loss of libido.[7]

Why not try Tantra as a gentle and meaningful connection to enhance your desire and experience of physical intimacy? It can be practised anywhere, at any time, and may just start to open the door to rediscovering intimacy between parents as lovers.

SO. YOU BOTH WANT SEX... BUT WHERE & WHEN?

Diana Richardson writes, *"You can engage in unassertive tantric sex in the vicinity of babies because it is a loving and natural happening..."*[8] We don't need loud noises or a thrusting bed to

---

[7] Diana Richardson, *Tantric Orgasm for Women*, Destiny Books, (2004)
[8] ibid

enjoy ourselves! A relief to every harried new parent.

A common question is whether bed-sharing or co-sleeping with your child(ren) prevents couples from having a fulfilling sex life? Well, there are many other locations around the house (and hey, making love in the car can make you feel ten years younger...) - just take the baby monitor and find a secret spot in the house... get creative! Remember and recreate the early days of snatching those illicit tender moments.

I like Tom Hodgkinson's (author of *The Idle Parent*) suggestion to just go to bed early. *"Well rested parents mean a more manageable day with the kids ahead as well as less irritated and snapping at each other parents."*

And, of course, that time can then be spent relaxing; if you feel like sex, great. If not, it can be equally satisfying and replenishing. In bed you can cuddle up, read, write, give each other a massage, read to one another etc. You are much more likely to be in the mood for sex when relaxed and emotionally close.

Avoid technical gadgets like a television in your bedroom; you want to nourish your relationship, not kill it, right? All digital devices work as a distraction. When used for work or entertainment they no doubt have their value, but in bed together you want to give your partner attention and spend time *together*.

Parents need to get creative and patient when it comes to sex. I certainly find that the less couples stress about it and accept what is and are honest with each other, the more they enjoy the levels of intimacy they previously had before baby's arrival.

Maybe you have decided to schedule in regular 'sex dates' in the week, just so that you get to have any at all. Or you feel that you are not ready for it just yet. Often just sharing the warmth of the other's skin is enough to recharge and get closer again. It's amazing what an old fashioned hug can do.

THE EMPATHIC FATHER

Whatever you decide, make sure you talk about it. Even if you are not on the same page, it helps tremendously to understand which part of the book your partner is at, and therefore how to catch-up when the time is ready.

I realised that sometimes Nedua and I were so occupied with caring for our children that we forgot the simple gestures of closeness that are so important and that we all crave. Holding hands, sitting on each other's lap, stroking, kissing, leaning against one another etc. are all little things that have a great impact.

Sometimes when we think we *need* sex, what we really need is some physical closeness and appreciation of our new roles as parents AND lovers.

Make a point this week to be intimate. Try something new than *just* having sex.

Also, think about other ways of getting the physical touch you need. I think many men shy away from physical contact with other men too much, or are only able to show affection in an aggressive way. Hug your friends, other family members, cuddle your pets, get a massage etc. I once heard that humans need sixteen hugs a day. Go and find them... well, you might want to ask first!

If you do feel like it, perhaps engage in slow sex that is geared towards relaxing together; do only what feels good. Don't expect an orgasm or think you *have to* provide one; obligation is an instant turn-off. Tell your partner what you like and ask him/her directly which way she/he wants to be touched. Let their hand guide yours. Try to totally focus on your breathing, on the touch you are feeling and stop your mind from wandering off (if it does, just come back to be present in the moment).

With pregnancy and birth your partner's body is going through big changes. Especially in the weeks and months after birth your partner's body may be very sensitive. Some women might hate their nipples to be touched, for example, but instead they would love a nice belly or foot massage. Also, keep in mind your partner's possible fear of vaginal intercourse (especially after she has had stitches), and for nearly all women a reduction in natural lubrication, hence the need to use more. Be gentle and creative and watch for signs from her when rediscovering one another. Your partner might also dislike her 'new' body or feel self-conscious or less sexy with the inevitable changes pregnancy and birth leave on the female body. Make her feel comfortable and beautiful, make sure she knows how in awe you are of her body having created and grown your baby and how you still find her attractive and sexy.

Intimacy thrives when we feel closely connected to our partner. Due to work and other commitments, that can be difficult for some couples to achieve. If you find yourself in such a situation do make the effort of taking small steps towards intimacy; it might take a little longer to feel closely connected again, but if you take time, if you start relaxing together rather than in front of something digital (or worse, separately altogether as you go to the bar and she goes to bed) you are on the right path.

Wherever you are at the moment you can still work at these ideas. Even if you feel sex is at the bottom of your priority list right now, it's still good to talk about how you want intimacy to look, especially if you have differing needs and wishes initially. You can come together again.

5. THE DREADED WORK-LIFE-BALANCE

Many parents find themselves with the dilemma of how to organise their lives. We want to be great parents and still have time for our partners. To fully nurture our relationships, and yes, to succeed in a great job that we love would also fit in nicely.

Often with the birth of our first child, many fathers like you and I have high expectations of ourselves: we want to be a great parent, a great partner and have a great career. We are being told that this is possible; it just needs some organisation and time management. Easy.

But is that true? We can't really have one without compromising the other.

Or can we?

In the traditional model (one partner works full time, whilst the other part time or is a stay-at-home parent) usually the full time worker does not get to spent as much time with their children as they would like. Many parents do have the wish to work less and to spend more time with their children.[9]

Our children need us, *both* parents. If you would ask children what they want from their parents, I think the answer might be for them to come home from work less tired and stressed. To have more time to play, read stories, and be there to witness their everyday achievements. Children need us to give them attention and love, but at the end of a long working day that's hard. We are exhausted. We rarely have sufficient energy or patience left after dealing with the demands of our days, exacerbated by the additional level of stress, exhaustion and sleep deprivation of being new parents.

---

[9] http://www.bbc.co.uk/news/education-26274518

THE EMPATHIC FATHER

When 'having a career' means spending fifty-plus hours away from home a week, relationships with our partners and children suffer; equal parenting and sharing responsibilities effectively is impossible in that situation.

Many will argue that they simply cannot afford to work less. I strongly believe employees should be given an incentive to work fewer hours. I am not sure whether it's as easy and realistic at the moment as it should be, given current attitudes and welfare infrastructure; both need re-prioritising in my opinion, although some countries have a much larger financial support package for families than the UK or USA.

I wonder instead whether we need to re-think our lives and jobs. At the moment most occupations are simply not family friendly.

They do not:

- Allow fitting working hours around family life

- Allow working from home or other remote/flexible access

- Allow taking time off easily and spontaneously when needed to care for family members

- Allow enough down time (and that means no work emails, late-night phone calls etc.) to spend with family

We as a culture remain stuck in the conservative model of 'your boss decides your hours and there is not much room for negotiation'. More and more of us are getting frustrated with that situation. We want to be in control of our lives and our children's upbringing.

I believe to achieve a well-balanced life we need to prioritise our family life over our work life, rather than trying to build our expectations (of how we want to parent and live as a family) around our busy lives and a box-standard career.

THE EMPATHIC FATHER

This is a scary thought. It means coming out of your comfort zone. It means going against the stream of people who think 'you can't do that,' - who would never dream of leaving a well-paid job just to have time to find out what you really want in your life and pursue it?

Well, I guess I will be ignoring their advice.

I'll be honest with you: My wife and I haven't found the ideal solution, yet. We've tried different work-life-family-models (like one works full time and the other stays home, or we both tried working from home), but we also acknowledge the fact that we have to pay rent and bills. We are both convinced that we are happier in ourselves the more time we can spend together as family and partners. That's why it's always worth to me to search for better ways than the standard.

Yes, you can choose to work a fifty-plus hour week and that might give you a certain security, primarily financial. I think less is more. Less money but more time for my kids. Especially with them being young at this moment, now. Career?

Personally, not as important as my family and the joy of experiencing my part in that.

If you aren't in a position to be at home full-time, do consider ways in which you can make your week more flexible. Could you work at home for part of the week? Could you cut your commute, or have dedicated 'no email' time at weekends? Could you discuss a pro-rata part-time arrangement with your organisation, or consider a sabbatical either around the birth, or when your partner's maternity leave has finished? Is there a way for at least one of you to be home full time?

Work is not all it's cracked up to be. There will always be more work, but you will never get this time back with your children. Your company could fold tomorrow leaving you without this all-important job, don't make your role in your family redundant in the meantime.

PART ONE AT A GLANCE:

- Try to understand and appreciate the changes your partner went through in becoming and being a mother. Not only has her body changed, her mind has a tremendous new focus. Respond with empathy, listening and support.

- The opposing demands of work and family can feel stressful, as there isn't enough time for either and you end up being tired and exhausted. It is important for you as a father to take some time to recharge too. Once your child is in bed, can you make time to do something you love? Don't feel guilty doing it, your partner needs you to be fully recharged, as much as she does herself.

- You might feel that no-one at work quite understands how you are feeling. Men need to offload too. Some find it difficult to ask for help, especially with emotional issues, but please do. Find someone you feel comfortable with (a friend, a relative or a professional) and let go. It will be a great relief.

- Be with your baby. Hold your baby, sing to them, wear them in a sling or cradle them whilst they nap. Be present. You are indeed needed, every single moment.

- Spend as much time as you can with the baby and don't be offended by your partner if she suggests you do things differently. The more you do, the more confident you get.

- Don't ever underestimate the importance of you being around. This is a critical time for bonding with baby and re-connecting with your partner as you redefine your growing family.

- Start talking to your partner and explore your own childhood. See what exactly happened there and how your past effects your present. Reflect on how you respond in conflict or in heated arguments. How do you cope with anger and frustration? Get this sorted ASAP. Start by talking to someone close to you about it if you can. There is always external support available, should you require it, and ask for it. I know men who have received help through anger management courses and workshops for example, but there are a range of services out there to support you, if you only look for them.[10]

- Meet with your own parents, particularly in this context your father. Find out about your first days and weeks. Listen to their stories without judging them. They might give you advice you don't want to hear. Let it be. You don't have to follow their suggestions, but you can see them as another possible way to approach situations, or enhance your understanding of why you might react in the ways that you do.

- Enjoy it! It goes all too quickly.

---

[10] Some suggestions are provided in the rear of this book

SOMETHING SPECIAL TO TRY: ONE

Write the birth story of your child into a journal.

Describe how you felt when you saw your partner being in labour and when the baby was there. Be honest with all your emotions and feelings. If you like add some drawings, clippings or keepsakes; whatever is special and memorable to you about the occasion.

Keep this journal and re-visit it whenever you like. It might be a great present for your child's eighteenth birthday.

.

PART TWO: YOU & SOMETHING DIFFERENT

6. BEING THE AUTHENTIC FATHER FOR YOUR TODDLER

...even when he calls you stupid.

"Stupid Papa."

That's the latest delightful expression my youngest son (who is just three) says at the moment. Sometimes it changes to *"Stupid Mama"* or *"Stupid Drawer"* (that was today when he squashed his finger)... but it's me who is more at home than Mama at the moment, so I usually get the *"Stupid-Papas."*

Lucky me.

I have been hearing this recently probably twenty-five times a day. I know very well that he doesn't mean it and that he has no intention to hurt me or; in his case today, the drawer.

He copies that word without understanding its meaning. And most of the time I feel relaxed about it and smile back. But it can also be very annoying and hurtful, especially so when I have a day when I feel low, sad or stressed.

The twenty-sixth 'Stupid-Papa' is the one too many. I could either scream or run away or firmly say *"No, I'm not STUPID. Eat your dinner!"* Or... I could take a short break and relax. Up to me, ultimately – but my reaction will profoundly affect the mood of the house, and whether my son is likely to burst into tears (or me). However, when I'm really stressed it's hard to remember that.

So, I had such a day recently. I felt a bit down and was browsing the net - blogs, articles, comments and so on - written by dads, health professionals or journalists. After reading an overwhelming amount of material I was feeling even more down.

THE EMPATHIC FATHER

So many people talk about fathers as heroes, super-cool daddies, all-rounders – you name it. Dads with their baby in one arm, at the same time on the floor playing hide-and seek with the other two, checking their work emails and on top of that – smiling. Yeah. Daddy Cool.

Or, in places I found the complete opposite: the total loser. The dads who have no plan at all. The ones who touch nothing because they're afraid to fail, or to upset their partner. Those who can't find their way around a nappy or an iron, let alone thinking about what to have for dinner. As my hairdresser said today (after she discovered that I am a fatherhood advocate), *"oh my, there are so many dads who have no idea whatsoever."*

Thanks, that's exactly what I needed.

I actually feel a bit sorry for both archetypes – and sorry for myself. I can admit that I'm rarely in the echelons of Daddy Cool (even when I actually do manage multitasking) yet I'm not sitting there clueless or uninvolved either.

Critically however, I don't want to believe in those stereotypes. On that particular day in my melancholic browsing I was looking for some authenticity. *Some simple, honest words.* I don't need the big show heroes to look up to, or conversely to read sob-stories of chaotic catastrophe to feel better about my unwashed dishes. Those stories might help some bloggers to increase their web traffic, but they certainly don't present the reality of fatherhood, and never helped me to solve a single parenting problem.

***

So, what do I mean by 'authenticity'? Parenting without a mask. Living with our feelings and showing our emotions. Expressing what I think and being clear on what I want. Yes, my children should see how I feel and how I deal with it. How else will they learn to do the same?

When I experience a very challenging and stressful moment, I try to tell my kids and my wife. They need to know. Yes, it should be time and age appropriate. It doesn't make much sense to explain to your nine-month-old that you've had a very hard day and that you feel exhausted and depressed, but you know what I mean. Sharing thoughts and feelings are the foundation for my children to grow up in confidence and with self-esteem. They know it's OK to have a bad day; it's absolutely fine to cry and to be sad, angry or helpless.

I learned to accept that I didn't need to fulfil any cliché of either super hero dad or complete loser at everything childcare or domesticity related. Instead, I needed to find my own new identity as a father and man. What type of dad would I have wanted as a child? Which values and beliefs do I want to give to my children on their way into adulthood? What kind of father am I able to be when I try my hardest? What do I still need to learn to be that father I hope to be?

Reflecting on these questions helped me to become more authentic in my parenting. I learned that it is ok, to say "*Hey I made a mistake here, but I am trying very hard/work on myself, so that next time I will react differently*". I don't need to feel a failure when a situation pans out differently to how ideally it would have. As long as I make myself aware of it, reflect on it and know that next time I need to challenge myself so that the reaction/planning/organisation in a similar situation will be a different one.

Children constantly copy us; often their behaviour is just that – a mirror image – of how we are feeling (and often we don't even notice what we are communicating unconsciously). So, when we are being open about how we are feeling inside and own up to these feelings, make them our own responsibility, rather than our child's (*"I am only so mad about that situation/in this moment, because you..."*) – we teach our children to also become authentic. Sharing their feelings so that we, as parents, and others are more able to understand them (and hey, understanding why your children do x, y or z is a wonderful thing!) and they us – this is the basis for empathy.

By consistently communicating in this way I began to witness little miracles. Just recently I felt a bit tired and slow. Then my six year-old came up to me, gave me a hug and asked, *"Are you OK?"* I never *taught* him that, he observed it many times and naturally understood.

So being an Authentic Father is the way forward for me. Talking about emotions inside me and to observe and react to what others think and experience.

No heroes, no losers – just people.

That's dads included.

7. WHEN YOU FEEL REJECTED

"I don't wanna play with you. I want Mama. She is more fun than you, I like her best!"

I'm sure many fathers have heard their children saying those or similar expressions. And even worse, often they come out of the blue with no warning, or any justifiable reasons.

It doesn't matter here if your kids are three or thirteen years old. When I heard those words from my eldest for the first time they struck me like lightning. I felt like dropping dead. Why did I get such a smack in the face? I try my very best as a father, every moment, every day. I play with them, I sing with them, we chase each other over fields – and then I get such a bill. Charming.

Often fathers' first response is: *that's not fair*! We feel mistreated, misunderstood and excluded. Mummy can do what she wants; she'll even get away with murder, but the kids will love her. I'm sure Mummy would swear it was the other way around, too.

Furthermore, I know dads who really struggle to spend time with their offspring on their own. Sometimes it's that they feel very disconnected from their children (perhaps because they are involuntarily less around, or perhaps even in some cases they hide themselves behind work and other commitments). For other dads the issue is that they are unsure of how to play with their children. Here I can warmly recommend Larry Cohen's book *Playful Parenting*.

Some fathers are eager and waiting to be needed, but on occasions it's the kids themselves who refuse to be without their Mom. Those dads told me how awful it is to feel rejected and unloved, especially when they have made a special effort that is not seen to be reciprocated or appreciated.

So, what to do? When I hear such words, thrown at me, I try to stay calm. Yes, it's an emotional heart breaker, but those words are not meant to hurt. What? But I just heard them crystal clear, they sounded pretty hurtful to me. Yes, but the message behind the words is a different one.

Let's take a look here:

- For quite a while most children will have a deeper relationship to their mother than their father. It all started in the womb where the bonding between mother and child began. Once born, that relationship gets deepened through breastfeeding and the very close time mother and child spend during the first months.

- Equally as important is the time parents spend with their kids. But even with currently two hundred and thirty thousand stay-at-home dads in the UK[11], it's more often mothers who are the main carers. So the kids often will feel more connected to her.

---

[11] http://www.bbc.co.uk/news/uk-26900543

■　　When our children tell us they like Mum better, they are NOT saying they don't love us. It could be just an expression of preference in that moment, or an outburst of frustration and anger, or it could be a coded message saying: "Dad, I want more time with you."

Confused about the last one?

Well, reflect on this: how often do you use negative/upsetting words when you're angry with your partner? When we speak like that we are actually calling for attention, saying, "Hey, I'm really cross, help me!"

Our kids (especially when little) won't say 'help me.' They can't verbalise those complex emotions, particularly at troubled times, but they touch your soul and feelings nonetheless.

Again, I try to stay calm (yes, that can be a hard job), then I try to see the actual message. Is my child upset about something other than what they are overtly yelling at me? I know rationally to remember about not taking it personally. I try my very best to be empathic (offering a hug – and again, don't feel rejected if they do not accept physical reconnection at this point) and see what I can do to offer comfort.

Comfort could work like this - I might say: *"Hey, Mama is not around at the moment, but we could play that game you really like, and later we'll go and find her."* Or perhaps instead, *"I hear you're missing Mum. Shall we finish this book and then tell her how much you love her?"*

Just remember, it's not your fault when children have moments like this, and there's nothing wrong with you (as a father, man, caregiver etc.). With my eldest I can say that his phase of 'I-Want-Mama-Now' has passed, more or less. But here and there I'll get the occasional *"Don't Like You."* Well, I look at him and say: *"Oh boy, you sound sad. Remember yesterday? The great time we had in the woods, making a fire and telling stories? I really enjoyed that time together. And the thing is, I love you very much."*

And deep down, I do know that he loves me too.

8. HOW PUNISHMENT DESTROYS TRUST

What a lovely afternoon we had today. The kids have been playing at a friend's house, for the last two hours (yes, it does feel like a short holiday). Don't you love days when you can let them run around and play hide-and-seek all day long, so that they can fall into their beds totally exhausted and get a sound night sleep?

Inevitably, our fleeting harmony was disturbed. My eldest came back home from their play-date, and I, habitually, checked with him if everything went OK. He looked at me and in his childlike innocence said, *"Grace can't meet me next week. She has said the F-word and is not allowed outdoors for one week. Papa, what is an F-word?"*

What a whopper. Suddenly I had two problems on my plate and wasn't quite sure what to say.

Not wanting to condemn Grace, or my understanding of the situation, I tried asking some more questions... *"Is she really not allowed to come out for the <u>WHOLE</u> week? Have you heard that word before? Are you sad that she won't be playing with you?"*

Basically I tried to buy some more time to think, but also to see how my six year old would deal with the situation himself. Markedly however, I was struck by the strong response Grace had received from her parents.

So, let's check this out. What had happened and why had her parents reacted that way?

Grace, a lovely six year old girl, had probably heard the F-word before; she must have heard it from somewhere in fact. It could have been anywhere - at school, from friends, through the media... or, let's be honest, maybe even from her parents themselves. Who knows? I have no idea whether she can link any meaning to the word, apart from the fact that many people use it for various situations in common adult language. I mostly assume that she simply had no idea what she had copied.

Very evidently by their reaction to Grace's expanding vocabulary, her parents don't want her to use that word, which I can completely understand. They probably felt embarrassed or even ashamed by their daughter's language (personally, I would feel the same). Furthermore, feeling trapped in that very uncomfortable social position they felt helpless and insecure. To make it clear to Grace, a harsh reaction was given, to — from their point of view — set a boundary.

Only when you reflect on that response, you will see the difference between boundary setting and *punishment*.

Why? Well, let's see how Grace might feel in response to her parents' actions. She could think the following: *"OK. I said something which Mummy and Daddy found quite upsetting. I'm not sure why, and what's so bad about that word. But anyway, I'm really cross now because I'm not allowed to play with my friends. And that's NOT FAIR! They are MEAN!"*

Grace would likely be confused, angry and upset about this punishment. And hey, wouldn't you feel the same? Let's assume Grace's Dad had said something inappropriate (which I bet he has done at some point in his life), either on purpose or by accident. Let's stick to the F-word in question.

So, he used it in some context. *"F***."*

Could you imagine his wife then saying to him, *"So, that was very naughty Jon. No sex for the coming THREE weeks. Go to your room and think about your behaviour?"* Would Jon really reflect on the words he chooses in future, or would he feel the same as Grace; confused, angry, upset? Does the punishment really fit the crime?

Will punishment really help Grace to understand what emotions the use of the F-word can trigger? I believe not. The only lesson she has learned is: *I don't trust my parents because they can be mean to me.*

And how often do we use those 'little' punishments when we think our kids have stepped over a line? How many times might we resort to bribing them in order to get their obedience? This is most basically every time we use an 'if → then... sentence'. *"IF you clean up your room, THEN you can have the chocolate."* Instead of co-operation and mutual respect, we (and yes, that's me often too) bribe, threaten or dictate. It's sad, isn't it?

Do we have a choice? Oh yes. Life often comes up with more than just one answer or one way to go. I like to use my *Listen-Empathise-Speak* approach, which I have tried out many times to surprising effect.

Here's how it works:

ONE: Listen to your child

(Or partner, friend, colleague...) Don't judge or jump to conclusions. Focus on the words only. The words themselves don't hurt you or me, they just transport a message. So, when your child — and let's go back to Grace's case — says the F-word, listen carefully how, to whom and in which context the words are being said. Was there a genuine attempt to shock, or cause harm? Was your child experimenting with language, with sound, or with your reaction itself?

TWO: Now pause, reflect and empathise.

Ask yourself the following questions: What is she feeling? Is she angry or upset about something? Does she really know what she's saying? Where could she have heard that word before? And go a step further by asking yourself, *"Do I use that word myself from time to time?"*

THREE: Speak

It could sound like this: *"Hey Grace, I just heard you say a word. I'm not quite sure, if I heard right. Did you say F***?"* — Wait for response — *"Ok, I just wanted to check. Well, I really don't like that word. I think it's very impolite and I know it can make people upset. And I don't want people to get* *upset. Not you or me or anyone else. Please tell me too, when I use a word you don't like, OK? Would you like a hug, before you go outside again?"*

See, how powerful your words can be and how they would solve the problem by talking or responding like that.

1. You address the problem
2. You don't judge
3. You explain your issue around the problem
4. You say what you would like for the future and at the same time you give your child a clear cue
5. You don't overpower your child by punishing; actually you do the exact opposite by empowering him/her
6. You're authentic by admitting that you sometimes too say mean words. Or simply: you are authentic.

Sounds like magic? Well, it's not. It's a great tool in dealing with problems. Yes, it takes time, reminding and reflecting to become confident in using it. But you'll see the differences and your child will be grateful (maybe not now but in twenty years perhaps, or when they become parents themselves).

And yes, I have to remind myself too, every day and especially in the heat of the moment. But it's worth it.

9. STAYING CALM WHEN YOUR KIDS FIGHT

"That is mine!"

"No, it's not!"

"Yes, it is!!"…Voices are getting louder.

"NO, IT – IS – NOT!!!" You can tell they're screaming now, back and forth, and rapidly escalating.

"NO!!!", "YES!!!!", "NOOO!!!!", "YESSS!!!!!" Quick slaps are getting exchanged, and at least one is crying by now.

OK, let's pause here. You can perfectly imagine how this dialogue will continue or further escalate. We've seen it so many times and we probably felt that many times annoyed, frustrated and helpless by watching it. And how often would we just march into their fight, tell them off, threaten them with ridiculous punishments (if you don't stop then there won't be any ice cream tonight) or shout things like *"Stop Now!"* in absolute desperation.

It's the sort of thing that happens every day, and yes, all children who are siblings will do it: they will fight. Sometimes more, sometimes less. Depending on their age and life circumstances, our lovely, cuddly, cute offspring will shout, scream, rage and try to hurt each other.

So, how should you and I respond? Which tools can we use in order to feel confident and secure in our response, rather than helpless and angry?

Check this out:

- At first, and I believe that is THE most difficult task, stay calm. Yes, take a deep breath and try not to jump in with full adrenalin that makes you feel as high as a kite. This way it's quite likely that your response is shouting, telling off or even physical intervention (which invariably ends up harsher then you *planned* to).

- Don't take sides. It's so easy to blame and punish, isn't it? If you make one child taking the blame and responsibility, then it will come back as a boomerang. Next time the non-guilty child will use that card as *"See, he/she does it again!"* It also pits one off against the other, which breeds resentment, jealousy, perception of your 'favourite', or fostering sneaky behaviour in order to not get caught and avoid punishment, which they would prefer their envied sibling to receive.

- If someone did get hurt, do pay that child attention and give comfort. Whatever had happened before doesn't matter. Physical pain needs your attention, your comfort and love. This models to the other child empathy, and a more appropriate way to act/react.

- Depending on your children's ages, you could ask them to try to find THEIR own solution for the problem. It could work like this: "*I see you both like playing with toy XYZ. I'm sure you'll find a way, so that you both can enjoy it.*" (Sounds impossible? Give it a try. Children can surprise you in their maturity). This encouragement can help your children to take responsibility and to get creative at problem solving.

- The 'We Share Our Toys' approach might be right from your point of view, but especially for smaller children the concept of sharing is far too complex. After all, if you were on your laptop or guitar and your wife suddenly demanded it was her friend's turn as a guest in your house, you might be peeved yourself. Arbitrary turn-taking is just that; arbitrary. We should share because we want to, because we appreciate the joys of playing together or making someone happy by offering a turn with a treasured toy. Most children prefer to engage in parallel play (that is, with their own object alongside another, rather than actively interacting) until well into pre-schooler age or later. Around the age of three they are able to understand this idea a little better, but even as adults we don't always get it right.

- Try to listen to what BOTH (or however many children are being involved) children have to say. Avoid questions like *"Who started it?"* — that leads to nowhere. After you've listened to them, empathise and give feedback like *"Yes, I can see that you wanted toy XYZ as well as your sister."* Smaller children (and older) often find it difficult or are just unable to express their feelings. So, help them by reflecting: *"Oh, you look very angry/upset/sad..."* This can help them to get a connection to their inner feelings, and gives them the language to express their strong emotions other than physically lashing out.

- When you see that your children can't solve this on their own and that they need support, you could:
    a) join in their game to take off pressure

b) ask them to take turns (with you present for guidance and support)

c) offer something completely different, e.g. *"Ok, I see that you are both struggling with sharing that toy at the moment. Let's put it away for now and go outside for the XYZ game you really like! Are you coming?"*

Whatever you'll choose from that list, try to be authentic. Remember we all struggle from time to time and even as an adult I find it difficult to share certain things at certain times. Just to give you another example: imagine you're sitting on the sofa to read your favourite book, then suddenly your partner comes and grabs your book with the comment *"It's my turn now, you've had five minutes."* How would you honestly feel?

Let's show some empathy for our kids – the results will be awesome.

***

And because there is quite a bit of negativity about siblings out there, I want to end this chapter on a positive note (which far outweighs the negative but just does not get mentioned enough).

I think having siblings rocks. They learn a huge amount from each other (one is good at x, the other at y – they are a model for each other), they learn how to care for another, how to take responsibility and how to interact socially in all the weird situations of life.

When the older one reads the younger one a book my heart opens, when the younger cares for the older one, takes his hand... my heart opens.

They truly can get along, despite the inevitable squabbles of any people learning to live together in the world. The important thing is to not pit them against each other, to not set them up to fail, to not treat them differently because of age or gender.

The key is getting your kids to co-operate at an early age. Get them to truly care that the other is happy, content, and loved. Fairness is not so much about treating everybody the same, but in making sure that everybody gets what they need.

And after all, who better to have your back than your brother or sister? Even if they did get an extra five minutes with that toy that one time.

10. GET LESS DISTRACTED AND BE IN THE PRESENT

For the last five minutes (or even longer) my eldest has being trying to explain to me the difference between elves and fairies. Or was it gnomes and dwarfs? No, definitely something with wings and a magic wand. Gosh, I lost the plot. *And that's not my son's fault.*

Whilst he tried to engage with me, I was miles away thinking of another blog post I could write, or some emails I should answer or the need to reflect on what Nedua and I discussed this morning...

In short, my day dreaming was about nothing consequential, or really, nothing as important as him trying to connect with me in that moment. I got distracted and lost focus and interest with what my child is telling me.

I confess this happens a lot to me. I feel like I am living in a world full of distractions. Not only my thoughts, but too often digital devices and that constant urge (yes, call it addiction if you like) to check them. We don't own a TV and I use my mobile phone only for making calls and sending text messages, so no social media and the perils that brings, but I still find myself in front of our laptop, checking emails and so on, for at least three, four times (and, yes, some days even more often) a day.

There is always a good excuse to quickly check something. *"I'll only be there for a minute,"* and that minute turns easily into twenty, thirty and more. When I hear my kids calling for me for the tenth time (and by now their calls turn into annoyed shouts), I put the laptop on stand-by and rush down the stairs with a feeling of guilt and the hope that no-one has noticed for how long I 'just checked' my mails.

THE EMPATHIC FATHER

Distraction is not solely a problem of our modern world. Yes, it's so much easier now to get distracted, but even in a world without smart phones, internet and TV, people would find other distractions or addictions.

Parenting is tough. Good parenting even tougher. I believe parenting is about stepping back and watching, playing, guiding, understanding, listening and being present.

When our children feel they need to compete with digital devices to get our attention, then something is very wrong.

I remember the time when mobile phones entered our lives and how annoyed I got when I met a friend in a café and the phone would go off. The whole conversation got interrupted by a (most likely unimportant) message. Then it took me and that friend a while to come back to our topic and to tune in again.

And that's what's happening with my kids now. They want to show or tell me something very important (yes, for them it is!), and I'm not emotionally or physically available because I'm checking a message, or thinking of something else.

I basically annoy my children by my inattention, and then I get annoyed if they respond to my non-presence with behaviour I don't like. Great. In the end we're all frustrated and stressed.

It helps me a lot to get reminded of that. Not through subversive glances and blames, but through gentle, positive language. When Nedua says *"I think the children want to play with you now,"* or *"I can see the kids need you right now"*, an inner alarm bell tells me to stop and see what's going on around me.

Yes, sometimes I need more than one reminder to check in with reality, but normally it works well. It's also the gentleness without any judging or blaming (*"Why have you spent so much time on the computer?"*, *"It's not fair that the children always have to wait for you."*), that I prefer.

THE EMPATHIC FATHER

And then I set some rules for myself: For example on Sundays all devices stay off (with really just a few exemptions). So, no checking emails or updating the blog or tweeting or whatever.

Another rule is to set myself certain time slots throughout the day where I work on the laptop. In that time I can check my emails a hundred times if I want to. But when that slot is finished, it's time again to be present for my children and wife.

Yes, our lives are busy and we have to remember so much. Even daydreaming at times can be quite satisfying in itself, yet I think being in the present is also like a meditation. You focus on one thing, and if your mind wanders off you acknowledge it, and then return to your focus.

Some activities help me to feel more connected with my children and to stay focused. For example, time for rough-and-tumble. This great game is especially good over the winter months when we burn far less energy and calories than in summer.

This is how it goes: Turn your lounge into a roughhousing 'go-wild' area. Take cushions, pillows, mattresses, duvets, blankets and soft fluffy items to cover the floor, and remove all sharp, hard or dangerous objects. Then invite your kids for a good and fair session of roughhousing. Make rules beforehand (e.g. *"We don't hurt each other,"* or *"Stop means STOP!"* and don't overpower your kids.

Let them 'win', or at least let them be in charge. This way their physical energy gets burned, while their glass of emotional needs will be filled up. Need more inspiration? I can warmly recommend Lawrence Cohen's book *The Art of Roughhousing*. My boys love to horseplay (and me, too. I always feel ten years younger afterwards). It's a great way to physically connect and release tensions of the day in a safe space, together.

Another one is having a good sort-through your household possessions. *Gosh, how much stuff do we actually need?* The answer is always the same: *less than we think.* But cleaning or decluttering aren't fun? Well, you would think so. Yep, it doesn't help much when you shout with a grumpy face *"For goodness sake, clean your bedroom now or I'll scream my head off."* The thing is, you can make them fun with a little imagination.

Have you ever tried to turn the ugly cleaning into a little party? Get the vacuum cleaner out, turn the music up and invite your kids to a dance. The dishcloth becomes a magic towel and everyone home joins in the 'who-can-pick-up-the-most-books-and-toys-and-put-them-away-in-three-minutes-race.' Everyone is a winner. Make a pile of toys and things you and no-one else in your home need. Take the stuff to the charity shop or give it away. After the cleaning party you can all settle on the sofa with a nice mug of tea or coffee, perhaps even a well-earned biscuit.

I also think it's so important to focus on what it is your child is into at the moment. Learn from them about their favourite topic, animal or story character, and even if you find playing with/hearing about 'their thing' rather boring, show them you care about *them* by engaging with it, at least some of the time. Allow yourself to be present with them. Let go, be a child yourself.

Finally, a good way to leave all distractions and artificial toys behind is to go into nature. That's really the key for our family when it comes to living simply and focused parenting. Out there in the woods you don't need your phone (no reception anyway) and plastic toys would look like alien objects on the forest ground.

I feel so much better and deeply connected with my children when we spend time outdoors. Making fires (where it's safe to do so), building dens or playing hide-and-seek in the woods. Then I can focus on them, the great environment and also on me.

I have realised how much more I can enjoy an activity with my kids when I don't distract myself. I feel more relaxed, more connected, happier.

When the kids have grown up and I look back, I don't want to regret that I have missed many great moments in their lives because I was too distracted. Or as Gerhard Pretorius has said, "*It is through the small distractions that we lose our soul. You choose what you pay attention to.*"[12]

Pay attention to your family, and learn to enjoy the little things together. Entertaining your children does not have to mean spending money on them, but spending time.

---

11. WHEN OUR CHILDREN SUFFER FROM LABELS

I really thought that I shouldn't need to write about this. I believed that's no longer a topic of twenty-first century parenting. And, oh gosh, I was wrong.

I'm talking about the big gender nonsense in our society. It all starts by how we treat our children by putting them into categories of gender: this is what *boys* do and that's what *girls* do, this is what *boys* wear, this is what *girls* wear...

When working as a Community Family Worker, I came across this a lot: Mum thinks it's a good idea to buy their sons (and daughters of course) a doll to play with. Then Dad joins in and says: "*My son playing with a dolly? No way, he will get a new football, that's what boys play with!"*

A quick look into any toy shop will confirm this view. Toys are largely categorised — again, girls toys (pink) and boys toys (blue of course). Girls play with dolls, prams, skipping ropes and pink balls — boys will play with cars, toy guns, pirate outfits and blue balls. Girls' toys are frivolous, innocuous, and often image oriented (make-up, jewellery, princess-play). Boys' toys are physical, loud and often with violent undertones (war games, guns, wrestling etc.).

But what would happen if there were no longer such stereotypes? What would our unique children genuinely choose if media, marketing and shops ignored colour coding and artificially fostered preferences?

My boys are going through different phases of playing with dolls. When my eldest was about eighteen months old we gave him a doll. He took the doll, looked at it and then kissed it. This was followed of a period of time where he would go with dolly everywhere.

After about six months he suddenly lost interest in playing with his doll. We didn't do anything about it and that's how it is until now. He's now six and pays more attention to his soft toy rabbit (well, now he wants a real baby to cuddle and look after. I guess he has honed his fathering skills on dolly, now we can move to the next level...). His younger brother has taken over the care for dolly. He looks after her like a father would care for his child. And that's exactly what playing with dolls is all about.

Loving a doll is about caring for someone; developing social, emotional and deep communication abilities, fine motor and self-help skills. It's incredible what children explore and develop when they play with dolls: The list is long. To check out all benefits on playing with dolls, have a read at Mama OT's blog[13] - she is an occupational therapist with focus on play-based learning, irrespective of gender.

---

[13] http://mamaot.com/2012/11/25/why-kids-should-play-with-baby-dolls-yes-even-boys/

***

It's interesting to see, how kids respond to the artificial advertising of gender roles. When we went out for a small lunch the other day as a family to a seaside café, my son asked why there were little flags in the Panini with crossbones and a skull on it? Well, what's the answer to that? I simply went with the best answer I could think of at the time, *"adults think children like pirates, which might make them like their sandwich, and therefore, this café."* His response was, *"I don't like pirates"*. Indeed, why would you necessarily?

Sometimes explaining the adult world to children, especially the world adults create for children to enjoy, is extremely difficult.

The other day I came across an article on the web claiming that our children need gender specific toys as we otherwise deny them their natural identity. The author went on to suggest that if you give a girl a log and a knife she will make a doll while a boy will turn his log into a weapon.

Naturally. In my opinion, that's the greatest bull***t I've ever read on this topic. Unfortunately, it was published on a well-known parenting page. I do hope people took this sentiment with the pinch of salt that it deserves.

I've no idea how many children that 'parenting expert' has observed and played with. From meeting and observing hundreds and hundreds of children over more than a decade, I can assure you that a child – whether it's a boy or girl - will always create something he or she has on his or her mind in that very moment. Environmental factors and social conditioning do play undeniably important roles, but so often I observed boys (those ones with that stereotypical label of dirty, loud, strong, scruffy etc.) who in an instant would pick up a dolly or walk gently around with a push chair, because they just *enjoy* it.

And why wouldn't boys want to naturally practise for when they become a parent, just as girls do when caring for dolls? And why would anyone want to deny boys this learning? Don't we want them to become gentle, loving and caring fathers one day? What's that got to do with their gender identity?

Such role segregation is only based on our cultural stereotypes of what a man is/what a woman is. We should not project this onto our kids — let them be and play with what they like. Believe me, they know best what they need and who they want to be if we let them be free from cultural and social conditioning imposed on us by the media, advertising or people around us.

***

So what if we didn't have any 'gendered' toys? I believe our kids would just continue playing. They don't care about gender geared (they will go for the colours THEY like) or 'appropriate' toys. Hypothetically, if someone asked me why our son wears purple, red or long hair, I will say *"Why not? There is no law which forbids it, no rules about who is allowed to wear what."* I won't love my children any less for making decisions that run against the grain.

With no interfering from our side they'll figure out themselves which toys are fun and which are not. Some will go through colour phases of liking one and then another. Did you know that only a few decades ago all boys wore pink, and blue was considered a 'girls' colour? Traditions change.

So, next time I hear a father (or a mother) say that their son(s) shouldn't play with dolls, I'll just pick up one, sit on the floor and pretend to feed it. Then I will wait for the boy to join in the game.

Kids play with dolls – let them enjoy it!

12. TAKING IT EASIER…
OR, WHY IT'S GOOD TO BE BORED

It all started as a normal, typical, windy, rainy, grim (this list could be endless) day in February. It was just after breakfast when my eldest came up to me with that one special facial expression, we've all seen. And before he even opened his mouth, I already knew what he was going to ask me…

"Papa, what are we going to do today?"

From there we had a dialogue which repeats more or less every day, and perpetually goes like this:

Me: *So, what would YOU like to do then?*
Son: Don't know.

Me: *Do you wanna find something you could do and later on I'll join you?*
Son: But I don't know what to do.
Me: *Wanna finish the puzzle you started last night?*
Son: Boring.
Me: *What about going for a bike ride?*
Son: It's raining Papa!! (Yes, obviously I had forgotten that.)
Me: *Ehm.*
Son: I AM BORED!

If I don't come up with at least five super-duper ideas and plans to fill every single second between eight am and eight pm, his response will be the same.

"But I'm sooooooo (add as many o's as you like) *bored! What can we do?"*

I invariably sigh, and ask myself what we actually could, or *should* be doing?

THE EMPATHIC FATHER

Often, when reaching that point, I would play my joker card: *"Shall we get the train set out?"* Normally a win-win situation (as we both like playing with the train set), yet on that cold February day it just brought a dry and weak smile to his face.

Oh dear, this would be more complicated than I anticipated.

We played with the trains for about ten minutes, and then he unsurprisingly lost interest. So I needed a Plan B – quickly. But what would be my Plan B, when my normal Plan B wasn't working? My mind was spinning and I felt a bit desperate. Not a good way to get inspired, let alone inspire them to fun.

I paused and remembered the Taoist concept of WuWei: *Sometimes taking no action is an action.* Thank you!

I know that you, I, and millions of other parents face this dilemma at least once a day, or perhaps we're lucky if it's only once a week. Whether it's holidays, rainy weekends or you happen to be a home schooling, stay-at-home parent like me, there are a lot of hours in a day with small children to entertain. When my wife and I swapped roles and she went back to work, I had that vision of being the universal Super Papa. I can do anything and everything – nonstop – 24/7... right?

I pressured myself a lot: I thrust myself into great outings, craft activities (I hate doing crafts), even baking with my cake enthusiastic boys.

It was fun but incredibly exhausting at the same time. It took me a moment to figure out that this artificial time table, which I more or less created, and covered nine hours each day, was not needed and actually more destructive than helpful.

Then, through reflecting and reading (and here comes one of my favourite writers Tom Hodgkinson's *The Idle Parent* again), I found out how important it actually is to be bored.

THE EMPATHIC FATHER

Sounds odd? Well, that's what I thought in the beginning. Wouldn't I be neglecting my children if I didn't offer stimulating activities around the clock? Wouldn't they get frustrated, make big messes and smash up the house? Would I be considered a bad, irresponsible parent? You see, the guilt trip can make you feel wobbly and insecure in the blink of an eye.

So, what did I reflect on then? I remembered my own childhood: the long and quiet (and sometimes lonely) moments, when I sat in my room or by the window and did NOTHING. Staring out of the window, a bit of day dreaming, watching people and cars passing by... being bored.

At the same time I enjoyed exactly those moments. So peaceful and calm, so relaxing and refreshing at the same time. No one who would demand things from me, no squabbles with my sister, no solving of unsolvable maths homework (which I hated anyway), no arguments – just me.

Often, after I had such moments of boredom, I returned to the business of life refreshed and more energetic. While I had that breathing space, my creativity did some overtime and I came up with ideas and plans on what, how and why I would be doing things. Of course I couldn't really appreciate it then, but I can now.

I see exactly that sort of creativity and exploring in my eldest, when I give him enough time and space. Yes, at first he might feel frustrated or even angry (*"Papa, that's just not fair!"*), but once he's calmed down he gets active. He might start his own art-project or turn his bedroom into a post office, or record his own story on tape or video... the list of creative play, *after being bored*, is long. Sometimes I then join in, as the customer in his post office or by listening to his latest story telling. I don't have to invent everything for him. No, he's creative enough.

So, I let him go and explore, play and experiment, because this way he finds out for himself what he enjoys and what he would like to learn. Don't get me wrong, most days are filled with some sort of activities anyway, but now they come more from my children. Sometimes, I feel like starting some creative project for my own enjoyment (on the art table, in the kitchen, outside, in the shed) and the children will watch or join in, working next to me. And I also like the mornings where I wake up and I know: hey, there is NOTHING planned for today. Kids are so often overscheduled that they don't get a chance to breathe, let alone think for themselves.

We are lucky to live very rurally (which has its drawbacks too, obviously) and my children spend a lot of time roaming the fields. They build dens, nests, dig holes, build things with nails, play fishing in the pond, collect stones and the other day were even chased by some sheep.

Being able to explore their world makes them independent and rich in natural experiences that no adult could manufacture as well as they can themselves.

Don't pressure yourself too much with organising activities all day long. Leave your day in the hands of your kids and you'll see what kind of creative things they can come up with.

Most often, their ideas will be awesome!

13. SORRY KIDS. I MESSED UP! HOW TO APOLOGISE AND RECONNECT

Some days we just have shitty days of parenting, and today was one of those days. You know what I mean. It has seemed whatever I or the children have done, or anything that actually happened today, just sucked.

My eldest whined and complained about everything and anything: the food (too spicy), the weather (too wet), his toys (too boring), me (because I'm not reading the same book to him for the twenty-fifth time today). During all this his younger brother took a pair of scissors and cut open the toothpaste tube ("*No, it wasn't me!*"), sets the alarm clock for two in the morning (*"No, it wasn't me, really!"*), and finally managed to block our toilet with the lid of our coconut oil jar (*"No, Papa, it wasn't me. Told you"*).

To say it in one sentence: I COULD'VE SCREAMED!

The thing is, you can replace 'could' with 'did.'

Yep, the same guy who has just spent twelve chapters telling you how to be empathic, calm, relaxed and so on, lost the plot. Because I was upset, I was annoyed, I was actually f*****g angry.

There is only so much someone can take and yes, parenting also means that we have bad days. We're just human beings. Trying our best.

I love my kids, obviously. In an instant I felt ashamed and bad. Why didn't I respond with a nice smile and a phrase, like *"Don't worry about the toilet. Yeah, it's just fifty quid for the plumber, but hey, it's just money, isn't it?"* The bigger problem might instead be where we go until the loo works again? Perspective is everything; no-one had lost a limb or burned the house down. Yet.

But, as I said before, I didn't respond in that cool, calm and connected way. I messed it up. But, the good news about that, it's OK. No, it's not really desirable to shout and scream (especially when we're telling the kids not to) but it does happen. To all of us. More important than the moment of kick-off is the aftermath. What you do next is where the key lies for me.

When I look back at my childhood, I remember my parents being loud or shouting at me on occasions only. Like a short but intensive thunderstorm. Sometimes it was about nothing (at least from my point of view), and then the 'deserved' ones. What I also remember is the fact that my parents never ever came to me or my sister to apologise. It just didn't happen. Once the thunderstorm was over, life went on – more or less – as normal. Only my dad could be quite unforgiving for a long time (but that's a different issue).

What I'm trying to say is that they missed an enormous and important chance of reconnection. They left me with all my feelings of resentment, frustration and shame, alone. Yes, I might have done something I shouldn't have. Yes, I screwed up. Nevertheless I deserved love, support and kindness, because that's what all children need: unconditional love.

After their anger had vanished, they could have come to me and said something like *"Hey, we were really cross with you and that's why we got mad at you, but now we wanted to see how you feel. And we wanted to say 'sorry' for being so mad. Look, grown-ups make mistakes, too. It's sometimes quite confusing and hard to understand, even for us. Anyway, we wanted you to know, that we still love you! You are not responsible for our anger, it happened out of our own fear, insecurity and helplessness."*

What a powerful message that would have been. In an instant I would have forgiven anything. I would have cried and laughed at the same time.

Kids want to be loved. Of course. And, yes, they're not doing things to purposively upset or annoy us. If we think it's mischief, it often is a little cry out saying *"Hey, I'm here. Play with me. I need you now!"* But often they can't say it (because they are either too young or they haven't got the words yet). Children are born experimenters; little scientists sent to test the boundaries of acceptable behaviour as they learn how to integrate into society, and take it forward.

Let's go back to my shitty day. Yep, everything went wrong, and that included my response. When the storm had passed and things settled down, I went to see my boys. I looked them in their eyes and apologised. The apology doesn't have to be very long (in fact, small children have correspondingly small attention spans), but should show respect and empathy. I see the very moment of the apology also as a great example of authentic parenting. I'm authentic because my kids can see that I make mistakes. That's fine. Because I take responsibility for my errors, and model how to deal with them.

After that we hugged and cuddled and reconnected. Children forgive so quickly and easily. They truly love unconditionally.

The reconnection and healing process is always so important to me. Often I try to do something I know they enjoy, such as reading their favourite book or having a long cuddle on the sofa. Especially with my eldest I use the evenings before he goes off to sleep to talk about it again. He often needs more time to digest things in order to reflect and to talk about his feelings. Having that good father-son-chat really helps us both to find to each other again.

No, I'm not afraid to apologise and I'll always tell my children how much I love them, particularly after such a shitty day.

PART TWO AT A GLANCE:

- When your child is telling you that they like Mum better, they are NOT saying they don't love you. It could be just an expression of preference in that moment, or an outburst of frustration and anger, or it could be a coded message saying: "*Dad, I want more time with you.*" Give them that attention and time.

- Never take it personally when your child calls you 'stupid' or other names. The same applies to parent preferences; often smaller children feel closer to their mother for a period of time and that's fine. Don't forget YOU ARE IMPORTANT.

- Punishing your child(ren) doesn't teach anything; you are more likely to destroy the good bond and relationship with your child. Find out what's behind your child's behaviour and why she is acting like that. Respond with Listen-Empathise-Speak. Check whether you have said something that could have been misunderstood by your child (or partner), or what the real intention was behind their undesirable action, before deciding on a way forward together.

- Yes, siblings fight (sometimes). But, depending on their age, trust them to solve their own conflicts. Step in as a guide if you feel they're stuck. Don't take sides and listen to all parties with the same attention and care. If someone got hurt, give all your comfort to that child first to model empathy and true apology.

- Be in the present moment. Yes, all our new-world-devices can make our lives in many ways easier, yet in some ways harder. Distraction and play don't go well together. Don't let your child compete with your mobile phone as he will lose. Agree with your partner or older child about time slots, where you can check emails, social media or the latest recipes for family dinners.

- It's absolutely fine to allow your children (and yourself) to be bored. Boredom is space where we can recharge and relax. It's also a great opportunity to allow all kinds of creativity to blossom.

- Be open and able to apologise to your child. Yes, we all mess up from time to time. Life is tricky and we are allowed to lose the plot occasionally. Reconnection and apologising makes us grown-ups authentic and real. Get this sorted as soon as possible after you have blown.

SOMETHING SPECIAL TO TRY: TWO

Do you know the saying: When the children are happy, then the parents are happy too? I think that's right! Spend this Saturday with the motto: **Let the children decide.**

Yes, everything: from when they want to get up in the morning (hey, they might choose to stay in bed until lunchtime, so you have the morning to yourself), then the activities they choose for the daytime, their favourite food, to the point they decide it's bedtime (agreed, it could be later than normal).

Psychologist Oliver James calls this 'Love Bombing.' He says *"I developed 'Love Bombing' to reset the emotional thermostats of children aged from three to puberty. It gives your child a very intense, condensed experience of feeling completely loved and completely in control."*

He advises to have a go at 'Love Bombing' for a day or two or even a shorter period, followed by daily half hour slots devoted to it. He states that parents report a closer connection to their child and that 'Love Bombing' balances the child's behaviour and personality.[14]

I think it's awesome, and really does work with our boys when things have strayed from balance.

---

[14] Read more at www.lovebombing.info

**PART THREE: YOU &
SOMEONE CLOSE**

14. BECOMING A FATHER AND STAYING CLOSE TO YOUR PARTNER

Every couple strives for a happy and satisfying relationship in which each partner feels secure, valued and loved. It's just that sometimes in our busy days and sleepless nights, we forget how to connect with and value one another as we both desire.

When partners become parents their life together, as well as each of them as individuals, changes completely. This new challenge can deepen the family's sense of 'us' or the partnership can suffer due to the myriad of new factors influencing the relationship.

Why is investing in your relationship important? Why can't you start in a few years' time, when the kids are older, when you have more time, when you feel less tired? Aren't you both old enough to understand? To wait a while for your own needs, when a small child's needs seem so much more urgent?

From years of observations (and in supportive summary of much widely available research), I personally surmise that:

- When we feel closely connected as a couple, we help each other in being a better parent. Being filled with love means we can share it more easily with our children.

- The earlier you work on a problem, the easier it is to solve — your connection needs nurturing.

- You deserve living in a happy and stable relationship... it keeps you healthy too.

- You are a role model for your kids; they will take you as an example of how to lead a relationship when they are adults. Your expected tolerance for (un)happiness now can have immense impact on the kind of future partner your child may choose, and how they interact as a partner/parent in their own right.

If we want loving and supportive relationships with and for our children, we deserve to work on maintaining our own successful, enduring partnerships.

NEW FATHERS FACE DIFFERENT CHALLENGES

New fathers can feel rejected by their partners, because new mothers have naturally eyes (and capacity for dedicated attention) for their baby only. But also because many fathers spend little time with their babies (due to work commitments or because their partners don't leave them the space, or find it hard to trust them).

They may feel inadequate, unconfident and clumsy, assuming mum knows best. Feeling alienated from your partner and child is hard and very painful. This can trigger a downward spiral where many men seek comfort in external addictions (work, sport, television, food, drink, sex etc.) and therefore spend even less time with their family. Some then give up and leave emotionally or physically. We want to avoid this.

If you recognise yourself in these words it is important to address these issues. You need to look at and work with your own attachment issues, as well as establish a positive communication culture within your relationship. It is crucial to be able to talk honestly about your emotions and voice your needs and wishes clearly in order to feel heard. Your needs cannot be met unless you voice them compassionately and explicitly, and offer the same opportunity for your partner. This is the basis of Non-Violent Communication (see the work of Marshall Rosenberg for more detailed examples and work throughs).

THE EMPATHIC FATHER

Make sure to get your needs met, but don't just rely on your partner for it. Think about other ways of getting the physical touch and love you need (without being disloyal to your partner, naturally).

***

There are more and more women's AND men's groups launching, (or start one yourself), which many parents find a brilliant way to talk about their experiences. You may form close bonds with others; people often report making life-long friends with those with children at a similar age, or corresponding parenting philosophy to their own. Sharing your highs and lows of the early days in a supportive environment can help ease some of the burden of having to tend to our baby's needs, as well as our partner's, or our own.

We cannot change our past, nor should we. We are not doomed by what we experienced as children and later on in life, because we have the opportunity to reflect on and learn from these experiences. Sharing experiences of others can bolster us that we are not alone, we all face similar challenges. We may even be able to learn from others, and avoid the pitfalls our friends have successfully navigated.

COMMUNICATION IS KEY

Often in conflicts we totally lose our head, say horrible things and then it feels like we are watching ourselves from the outside. We are aware that we need to stop, but feel unable to break out of this part of us. Dr Sue Johnson (2011) writes that *"our deepest and most powerful emotions suddenly tak[e] over. Especially when our primal attachment needs and fears are touched by our partner."*

This can happen through almost anything, and something as little as a look or a facial expression can trigger an intense reaction in us. It takes less than two hundredths of a second to register the emotion on somebody's face.[15] And then we say *"he/she pressed my buttons and off I went."* We cast our own interpretation on often fleeting

---

[15] Daniel Goleman, PhD, *Social Intelligence: The New Science of Human Relationships*, Bantam, 2007)

instances, which can rapidly escalate into full blown misunderstandings and meltdowns.

When a couple is stuck in the disconnection cycle they often find themselves in roles where one takes an active role, whilst the other becomes more passive. In this model one partner may respond to discussions or arguments by partial or total withdrawal, for reflection to formulate their feelings, or eagerness to just let the matter pass. This usually manifests itself in their feeling inadequate, shameful or helpless, or even not responding to the other party entirely.

For their more talkative partner, frustration at not being responded to effectively or in the manner they expect/need, causes equal feelings of frustration and abandonment. Some people need to feel their partner is truly engaging with them in discussion; they need a tangible response they can 'work with' rather than the perceived hostility of silence, or unwillingness to re-discuss the same points in seeming perpetuity. The argument or underlying emotion/need then cannot be resolved/aired in the manner each would prefer, and as a result each partner feels misunderstood and disconnected from the other.

If you are caught in such a cycle, the first step is to acknowledge that you are; try and look at it from the outside. Map the conversations (fights) you are having on some paper to identify triggers, common themes that emerge, which roles you take in it, and how you go round and round and nowhere but into deeper disconnection. You could use arrows or timelines to try and visually demonstrate what happens, and how this vicious cycle is perpetuated. This is one of the most successful and powerful illustrations I have encountered to help demonstrate and diffuse the patterns we weave for ourselves.

It is hard to start looking at these fears and needs, but if you don't, you continue with this circle of anger, withdrawal or denial, defence, and more frustration and anger. Or to sum it up, it ends in feeling increasingly disconnected, which lessens our ability and desire to fix things. We each feel the injured party, and are unwilling to see or assume our portion of blame, or indeed how to move forwards, together.

There is simply no way around it. We need to open up, be vulnerable, and truly listen to the underlying needs each party are trying to communicate. Without this willingness and understanding, there is no enduring connection.

That's why it is so important not to dismiss a new father's need for reassurance and fostering connection between the parents as well as the father and child bond. We owe the same to our partners.

You need to try to identify your hot-buttons. What does your partner do, or not do, which provokes the greatest reactions from you?

You might be able to do that by thinking back to a conflict situation, an argument you had or simply the last conversation that didn't go the way you wanted to, where you got angry or withdrew, or perhaps where you felt distant to your partner.

To be able to connect deeply, we must learn to tap into our deepest emotions and then voice our needs clearly. Ideally this means without all the 'decorations' we often put on our words (i.e. past associations) and defensive actions to avoid being vulnerable.

Do you feel disconnected from your partner at this moment?

Well, to break the ice, try this:

Do something for your partner that she/he will love. Perhaps a massage, read her/him a story before bed, write a short love letter, cook their favourite dinner... step back, pause and feel the inner love for your partner. Remember to enjoy each other, as you once used to.

15. BEING CLOSE TO YOUR PARTNER
THROUGH ACTIVE LISTENING

How often do you argue with your partner and feel misunderstood? How many times do you respond with anger, defending yourself or becoming cross when she or he doesn't 'get' you? Close connection comes through really seeing our partner, understanding who he or she is.

Essential for that are active listening and empathy. Based on Stephen R. Covey's work[16] and that of other researchers, I have summarised how their findings can support your communication with your child(ren) and partner.

***

---

[16] Steven R. Covey: *The 7 Habits of Highly Effective People*, Simon & Schuster Ltd., 2004

WHAT IS ACTIVE LISTENING?

"Seek first to understand, and then be understood."
~ Stephen R Covey

In conversation, we are used to listening to ourselves in response to what the other person is saying. Realistically that means we merely 'listen' to our *reactions* to what the other has said, judging, commenting on it in our mind and formulating a response, and essentially only waiting for our turn to speak.

Most of us have a tendency to jump in and give opinions or possible solutions before the other person has really finished, and certainly without really understanding what they were trying to communicate.

Active listening however is when we stop focusing on our own agenda and thoughts and focus fully on our partner's words, intonation, body language and facial expressions.

When we truly want to understand, we need to listen actively, which means:

- Giving our full attention. This can be shown by moving our body towards the speaker, nodding or mirroring their body language, and putting away your mobile phone or thoughts about the football or office.

- We can repeat and summarise key words and phrases. Be careful to replay their words, so that you don't change the meaning of what they said.

- Reflect back the emotion that you hear them express, e.g. *"You sound very sad..."* However, it is important to not impose interpreted feelings upon the other person; you don't want to make the speaker believe he/she is sad, for example, if they are not. If in doubt, *ask them.*

- By paraphrasing what the other has said you encourage him/her to expand upon, or continue their position. When you both feel you have come to a point in the conversation where it might be helpful for you to interpret what has been said, this can be useful for the speaker to clarify his/her thinking.

The aim of active listening is that you are more able to truly understand the intentions of another person, and therefore feel yourself in his/her position to be able to respond with empathy and compassion. It also signals to your partner (colleague etc.) that you value and are seeking to genuinely understand them.

***

To practice active listening with your partner perhaps arrange a quiet evening, order or cook some special food and have a candlelight dinner (or anything more specific to you both that you know your partner will find romantic or will appreciate your efforts in creating).

Have a 'listening evening'. Give each person time to talk without being interrupted for five/ ten (you decide what feels best) minutes, whilst the other truly listens. Make sure you really pay attention and don't let your thoughts drift off (if they do, refocus and come back to listening actively).

Take what you hear as the thoughts, feelings and interpretations of your partner, rather than staunchly defending 'the truth' of a situation (their truth might feel very different to yours, both are valid). This means you avoid getting into justification mode (*"she always accuses me of this,"* or *"I never said that..."*), which shuts down the communication that you are trying to open.

Active listening means you look each other in the eyes; you can nod, you might want to clarify points, but the idea is not to butt-in, to steer the conversation to your agenda, or to challenge what the other has said.

Start your sentences with 'I', if that helps you to talk about your own feelings and interpretation, rather than be seen to be accusing your partner of something.

Get closer. Really listen to your partner, and have them really listen to you. Remember, retain and rediscover your connection by showing that you really care and understand what is important to you both.

16. GIVING IN.
NOT ALWAYS NEEDING TO BE RIGHT

Do you recognise the following situation?

You have an argument with your partner. You try to make him/her understand your point, you illustrate it, talk about your experience, you voice your feelings, and then provide supporting arguments for what you feel has happened.

Your partner listens and then tells you about their point of view, offering their counter arguments... Neither of you sees the situation, or way forward, in the same way. Neither of you are 'backing down.' *And why should you?* You are right and they are wrong, after all (?).

You're stuck. A compromise? No, why would you accept that? You are sure about your point and its importance and rightness. You don't want half a solution; you want and need reparation in full!

Some couples might then revert to using some 'verbal violence', just to get the other to **UNDERSTAND!** This could be blame; *"If you hadn't done x, this would all be different"*, or the use of direct accusations, generalisations and exaggerations. *"You never try to understand me…"* Or perhaps one of you decides to pull along others into the boat with *"it's always because your mum/ friend/ brother…."*

If that doesn't make the other concede their position and accept defeat, we might consider it helpful to elicit the involvement and opinion of others, so that we feel our argument gains in weight and importance. If you tell a friend or relations about your argument, usually they will agree with you (having only heard your side of the argument facilitates agreement, and you are more likely to speak to someone who you believe will be sympathetic to your position). This makes you feel stronger in proving your point... because Auntie Doris agrees with you, why can't your partner understand *NOW*? In all likelihood, he/she feels ever more disconnected and threatened, readying themselves into a position of defence or further attack. And so we go on.

What's happening here? What's the bottom line of this? Each of you is trying to prove their point; each naturally seeks to be 'in the right.'

At the beginning we might have tried to understand the other's point, to show empathy, but soon this becomes a full blown fight. Sometimes we even forget what it was all about in the beginning when we are so focused on being right in the end. A frontier has been built. It becomes a battle to hide the hurt and true feelings emerging, including memories of previous fights and unresolved insecurities.

The chance of connection – of achieving true understanding - becomes lost.

After all the quarrelling and trying to convince your partner of your point, it's hardly likely they will suddenly say *"Oh yes, actually you're right, why haven't I realised before?"* Even if they might secretly think that to themselves, in an atmosphere of violence and disconnection they cannot share that new awareness without feelings bubbling of having 'given up.' After all, you have been engaged in battle; it requires quite some self-reflection and strength to be able to recognise, accept and apologise for being wrong.

It can be hard to stop once you find yourselves in this downward spiral of disconnection. To prove your point or to make the other understand you lose your closeness, and weaken your connection to one another.

Next time you are trying to get the other to understand your point, or for that matter attempting to get your child to do something you asked for, ask yourself which direction you are taking with your words and actions; the way of connection and resolution? Or are you in fact building a wall between you, which gets higher and more insurmountable with each negative interaction?

When you are deeply connected you are able to show empathy as well as receive it. If nurturing the relationship between you becomes your upmost goal, you are far less likely to have the kinds of fights I have described. Instead, if you listen actively, if you ask questions, if you seek to understand and find a way that works for both of you (but doesn't feel like a half-hearted compromise), you may find your inevitable differences of opinion at times need not necessarily turn into escalating disagreements.

Often the way forward as a couple will be a lot clearer to you both once you have had an honest discussion, and had the courage to be vulnerable by allowing yourself to show your deepest fears and feelings. Our arguments mainly stem from inability to express or meet an underlying need such as warmth, love and security. 'Being right' is not a need, and having that badge will not satisfy whatever it is that you are really looking for from the other person.

Stop wanting to be right, and start wanting to be close.

17. BLAMING AND SHAMING
DO NOT HELP ANYONE

Blame and shame are usually big topics amongst parents. It's not easy to overcome the urge to criticise, especially nicely wrapped in a parcel of blame. We can spend a lot of time accusing the other, 'finding the culprit', but hey, love is not a detective novel.

I used to say things like: "*Nedua, our son caught a cold because you went outside with him without his hat on,*" or "*why didn't you tell me earlier that you've got an appointment? Now I can't do xyz.*" We all at times have said things along the lines of "*This has happened because you...*" or "*why on earth did/didn't you...?*"

Casting blame leads to arguments. Does it lead to the other thinking *"oh yes, of course you are right, I'll do that next time?"* Does it lead to warm fuzzy feelings about yourself or your partner? Does it solve whatever the issue was in the first place?

I think the answer is no.

If you think your partner *should* have done X, Y and Z (done the dishes, tidied up, phoned the bank etc.), but they haven't, then there is probably a reason for this, whether you think it's valid or not. If we believe the best or worst of a person, they tend to live up to our expectations. It is important to understand the reasoning behind what has happened before casting negative aspersions on the motivation or instance that led to your frustration.

At times, it's often easier to do the task yourself (without casting looks or moaning!). If you can assume they have done the best they could possibly do with what the resources, capacity or knowledge they had at the time. Maybe your wife hadn't phoned the bank because she'd been clearing up after the dog this morning, and then the line was engaged? Maybe your child was about to put away their bricks but got distracted by the dog, and then it was lunchtime and... after all, small children's attention spans are generously estimated to be *one whole minute*, especially when it comes to tidying up. It does not mean that they are inherently bad or doing/not doing something purely to irritate or make more work for you.

If you can do the task yourself, do. It would be very Zen of you to notice something needs doing then just take gentle and direct action to complete it without judgement or complaint. If you cannot for whatever reason do the specific thing that is needed, perhaps give the other person more time and a gentle reminder, or find out how you can help them achieve whatever it is that is needed (maybe there is another task you can do to relieve him/her?).

Don't ever let yourself fall into the trap of "*I have done more than you,*" and "*my day has been more stressful than yours*" etc. It doesn't help anyone, and your task is still unfinished.

Be forgiving and understanding. Catch yourself before you sigh or roll your eyes. We want to love our children unconditionally; I think our partners deserve the same.

If we *expect* of them to do certain things or behave a certain way, this is stressful for all concerned. And it does not change anything. Expectation is the mother of disappointment; years of moaning and showing disapproval will not have turned around anyone's relationship, I am quite certain of that. But what I do know is that it leads to resentment, to hiding feelings (or actions, for that matter). It creates an atmosphere of mistrust and inadequacy.

Instead, change your own behaviour. I am sure you know that you cannot change somebody else, they can only change themselves. If they want to. You are in control of your thoughts, not anybody else, or their actions.

You don't have to insist that "*they should have done the dishes.*" Instead you could think, "*I notice that we have a lot of dirty dishes. I'll talk to them and ask for support in some kind of way… No, hang on, everyone looks extremely tired right now. I think we can survive without them being cleaned immediately, and one of us can do them in a minute."*

Then a more gentle solution than shouting or blaming would be to offer something kind to your partner and do the dishes this time. You can have a discussion at a later point about why they weren't done, and why it was important to you that they were. You might find that after your loving attention and understanding of their day that your partner has found some new energy to get those plates washed.

If this dishes or dogs or blocks on the floor (whatever) becomes a persistent issue, meaning that you are unhappy with a recurrent behaviour of your partner, mention it in one of your 'Listening Dates' without any blame or list of criminal instances. Just talk about how you feel when you see a heap of dirty dishes each evening; it is important to find a solution together.

If you have a strong need for a clean kitchen, perhaps you could be the one 'in charge' of that aspect of clean up whilst your partner cleans up after the dog and kids? There is always a solution to the particular task in question, but the annoyance we feel at it not being done tends to be again more about you feeling that your underlying needs have not been understood or addressed by the other. 'If they loved me, they would know I like to come home to a clean kitchen, so they would've done the dishes like they promised.' The dishes themselves are rarely the issue. There will always be more dishes.

Striving for this level of understanding and new pattern of communication and reaction is all part of creating a culture of connection and loving kindness in your relationship.

Many of those inner needs, reactions to others and deep self-beliefs about our capacities and requirements stem from our childhood. It has helped me to look back and think about myself as a child from an adult perspective. I once wrote to myself as a child as part of releasing the sadness of not having been cared for more lovingly. Ask yourself, who gave you what you are aiming to give to your partner/children now? Get those feelings out, name them, feel them and see whether you can let go. This might include a need to be 'right' from past competition with your brother, or a need for order in the kitchen from your mother's insistence on immediately doing dishes after dinner.

I still come across my inner child sometimes; he usually voices his emotions in a heated reaction. Once I have calmed down, I can hug my inner child and remember more loving words. I can be grateful for being an adult who can move on. Apologise if others have been involved and then let go. Blame helps no-one; neither your partner, your child, nor yourself.

CHANGING YOUR HABITS OF NEGATIVITY

John Gottman developed *The Sound Relationship House* in his extensive work on couple's therapy. One of the stories of the house is called 'Share Fondness and Admiration,' in which he says: *"The fundamental process is changing a habit of mind from scanning the environment for people's mistakes and then correcting them, to scanning the environment for what one's partner is doing right and building a culture of appreciation, fondness, affection, and respect."*

This truly is a habit of many of us, however it also is *only* a habit, which means that you can change it. I did and so can you. Maybe not from one day to the next, but it is a way of life that is transferable to other areas of life too. I call on this to fight against my inner critic or 'worst-case scenario guy'. Many authors have written about the perception that the more positive you invite into your life by changing your thought patterns, your words and actions, the more positivity will come, and stay.

John Gottman's studies show it takes five positive experiences to make up for one negative experience in a relationship. That's five little acts of kindness for every annoyance, misunderstanding or hastily unkind word, so we all really need to get those positives flying around.

THE EMPATHIC FATHER

I think it is essential for this to work that you are as well rested as you can (tired and stressed people tend to be a lot less able to think rationally), especially in the early days of parenting.

So, rest when you *'should'* do the chores. Sleep when your baby does. Get some 'Me-time' wherever possible. It's important to do some exercise – even if only at home to a DVD, or take a walk together after dinner. Surround yourself with positive people who you like to be around, go out into nature, sit still and choose not to listen to the constant mind chatter, let it go and focus on your breathing, on the beauty around you.

Everyone needs these refuelling at times, to be able to offer the best of themselves.

Rid your world of criticism... which by the way includes criticising yourself. It will take some time, but life will be so much more enjoyable, believe me.

BRINGING UP AN ISSUE WITHOUT CRITICISM

When we feel the need to bring up *an issue*, often the rest of the conversation is hampered by the way we choose to start the conversation. It could start like *"You always leave it up to me to organise the kids' activities."* What kind of response will that elicit? Probably one of self-defence. We humans are good at it.

What other ways are there to start a conversation? How can you get what you want (talk about that issue) without criticising?

Start with how you feel. Use 'I', rather than 'you.' Ask questions. State exactly what you need, without blame.

"I feel stressed by organising the kids' activities. I feel I am not doing a good job at it at the moment. I need some help. Are you able to think up something for next week?"

Can you see that when instead of blaming your partner, criticising or accusing you start by talking about how you are feeling, it would elicit a more positive response from your partner?

Reflect whether the things you most criticise in your partner are things you actually want to change in yourself, your work, friendship group etc. Unfortunately, this is often the case.

And finally, when you catch yourself being hard on your partner or yourself, stop, breathe and then say sorry to them/yourself by being nice instead. Make yourself your favourite dinner, call someone you love and tell them about it. Do that whenever you think you have made a mistake and would otherwise get mad at yourself, for only being human.

18. BREATHE DEEPLY AND FORGIVE

We all make mistakes; it is part of life, and part of our learning journey. When the actions of another have hurt us, we can decide how to deal with it.

First of all, it is important to talk about the hurt in a non-judgmental way. Stating the facts: *"When I heard you say that, I felt..."* or *"This has triggered my fears of..."* or even *"I need you to..."*

By letting the other know how you are truly feeling, you open your heart for them to take your hand, apologise and hold you. Feeling held, you can start healing and connecting again. Forgiving is strengthening your connection, whereas harbouring resentful feelings will always lead to disconnection.

When have you last forgiven something of the person you love? How did it feel for you afterwards?

***

WHAT IS A PROPER, HEARTFELT APOLOGY?

It is healthy to apologise, for you and your partner. Recognise when you need to, and do it!

How? Start with *what* you didn't get quite right. *Why* that was, and *how* did you feel? *Acknowledge* how your partner must have felt in turn.

For example: "*I said 'I didn't care about you.' I am sorry, I was afraid to show you how I really felt. I felt helpless, lost and unsure of what to do. You must have felt hurt by my words and confused, because you know I really do care immensely.*"

Anything less is usually not a heartfelt apology, and is seen as that. It might be hard at first, but I promise it will get easier. With true reflection, openness and practice you will be able to get there.

***

Life is not like it was before baby or children. You would not be alone if you were at times struggling with the transition to parenthood, which is a gradual one, even though baby arrives with a bang.

Most new parents have financial, emotional or work worries. If you are a stay-at-home parent you might feel stressed that you are not contributing to the household income or overwhelmed by tending to the daily needs of your child(ren). You might feel undervalued and nobody seems to acknowledge how stretched, tired, exhausted and miserable you feel, even though you '*should*' be happy with your new baby. If you go out to work you might feel guilty, resentful or judged by others. You may feel a lot of pressure on you, being the main 'breadwinner' in the family now, with your growing family to support. Please know that other parents struggle exactly like you do.

It is not easy finding the right way for you and your family. You are allowed to change track to adapt things that fit your family and not feel you need to justify yourself.

If it feels too overwhelming, do ask for help. This can be a neighbour, friend, relative, or professional help. Even if it is just to come round and take the baby for twenty minutes, clean the floor, hang the washing out or cook a bit extra to share with you so you can stay well-nourished; this is essential for being able to master this demanding time.

If you like everything to be perfect, like me, you will struggle. Children certainly teach us to lessen our grip on household perfection.

Believe me, you are already doing an amazing job. Be kind to yourself.

Finally don't forget, even though it is hard to imagine when you are in the thick of it, this phase in your life will pass. It is a wonderful, unique time and if you work on it you can leave it feeling closer and more connected to each other than you ever were. Your kids will grow up, things will get easier (even though challenging in other ways), there will be nights without broken sleep, and as teenagers you will have to drag them out of bed. I promise!

PART THREE AT A GLANCE:

- Do something for your partner that they will love (a massage, read her/him a story before bed, write a short love letter...) especially at those times when you don't feel like it at all — that is exactly when you both need this connective exchange the most.

- Be honest. When discussing aspects of your relationship or difficulties you are facing, start your sentences with 'I' and talk about your emotions as being your own. There is nothing worse than saying, *"You hurt me when you went out with your friends last night..."* Own up to the fact that you are the maker of your own feelings and thoughts. Instead try *"I feel lonely at the moment and would love to talk to you about where those feelings are coming from."*

- Do acknowledge your partner's work (whether it's at home or out and about). There is nothing nicer than saying to your partner *"You look very tired, I can see you had a hard day today, would you like a hot drink?"* (And yes, you might feel like it's you who deserves that drink, but believe me, the more you offer kindness, the more it will return to you too).

- Schedule in special time. Some find that too prescriptive, however if you find you don't manage to find that time naturally it does help to know you have that dedicated space together. Special time can be just the two of you doing something you love. Get your favourite take away once a week, watch a new movie, read for each other etc. And yes, some couples also schedule in sex. If you feel this is at the bottom of your priority list at the moment, but still one of you is unhappy about this, talk about what you want your level of intimacy to look like.

- Have a *Listening Evening*. Each person has time to talk without being interrupted for a given number of minutes, whilst the other listens. Make sure you really engage with what they have to say and don't let your thoughts drift off (if they do, make sure you come back to listening actively). Take what you hear as feelings and thoughts of your partner, which are valid interpretations of events. Avoid falling into justification mode (*"she is always accusing me of this"*, *"I never said that..."*). Active listening means you look each other in the eyes, speak only to seek clarification or mirror their sentiments, and take time to process the needs that your partner is really trying to communicate behind their words.

- Share what you've been up to during the day, even if you think it's too mundane or boring to share. Talk about how you felt when X happened or Y said this to you. Being part of each other's day keeps you a part of each other's lives.

- Take time for yourself, even if it's only short. Go for a walk/jog in the park, phone/talk to a friend, go out for coffee, read a magazine/newspaper without being interrupted, go to the library, listen to an audio book, take a long bath etc. Everyone needs some 'Me time' to recharge batteries. Offer this opportunity to your partner also.

- If you think your partner *'should'* have done X, Y and Z (done the dishes, tidied up, phoned the bank etc.) but they haven't, there is probably a reason for this. If you can, try compassionately and gracefully completing the task yourself, or find out how you can help (maybe there is another task you can do, to relieve him/her). In our house we have a simple rule: If you see a mess, clean it up or leave it. But be happy with your decision.

- Sometimes it is good to accept the situation as it is. If your house does look like a mess at the moment and there is no time to clean up, you have to decide how important that really is in the grand scheme of things. If you have spent the day instead actively engaging and having fun with your partner and kids then that's what counts. You can have a clean house again... someday. But you cannot catch up on those magical moments between you and your children where you have fun and truly foster the bond you develop by being there for and with them. Kids make mess, but you can clean it up later, together.

- I know fatherhood/parenting can be a time of worries (financial, emotional, work worries, etc.). Believe me, you are already doing an amazing job; you are raising the next generation. The fact that you are reading this book (or any on similar topics) means that you care and want the very best for your family, which is the very best kind of perfection.

Finally, don't forget, even if parenting is one of the hardest jobs in the world, it is a wonderful, unique time. Allow yourselves to really enjoy that journey.

Create a Love Weekend...

... for you, your children and your partner.

It could work like this: Friday afternoon and evening is your time where you decide on what you would love to do, both with the kids and after they have gone to bed. Then on Saturday your focus is on the children. Make it their turn to be showered with attention and engage in things they enjoy doing. Finally, Sunday is your partner's big day. Make it special to them. You can plan out such a Love Weekend together with your family, or why not surprising them? In any case, it will feel good to take the time to pamper each other as individuals within a family.

FINAL THOUGHTS

Before I leave you to go and play with the kids, here are some closing thoughts.

This book was designed for all types of father in mind. Whether you are a stay-at-home dad or hands-on kind of guy, or not. Whether you see yourself as a hero, loser, career-machine, softy, workaholic or chocoholic. Whether you are the kind of dad to give mum a run for her money in the multitasking department, or can admit to being one of those clueless guys not able to distinguish a vacuum cleaner from a washing machine. Perhaps you manage to be the superhero-Papa, flying in between work and home life not letting any task slip past unattended. We are all dads trying our best to build and maintain a loving and close family, so I thank you for taking the time to read more about things that have certainly worked for my family, and could work for you too.

We have all seen the pedestal image we are supposed to be striving for as the 'man of the house'. Super-Dad himself. The impossibly perfect magazine-man, whose gym body sits comfortably in the managing director's seat of the big name company, and who coaches his children's sporting team on the weekend. Before his conference call, Daddy Cool always finds time to check in with his model-wife to surprise her with dinner in the most expensive restaurant in town. And, oh yes, spending quality time with his four young kids, who each have soccer, maths club and a private language tutor before a seamless bedtime routine and the babysitter arrives.

Sure, if you are only successful enough, smart enough you can have it all...

Perhaps I should confess something has gone completely wrong in my life. I look nothing like this image of domestic paternal perfection.

But wait, what if this image actually bears no resemblance to the kind of father that I actually want to be? What if I don't buy in to fatherhood as it is in the movies? What if I decide *not* to be

Super-Dad, and just be a dad who is super all in my own way?

What if I decide to make spending time with my family the priority in my life? What if I decide that because I love my kids and my wife, I am not going to work forty or fifty (or more) hours a week? What if I decide that I am not going to let my life be controlled by a big corporation? What if I decide that I am not going to work for far less than I am worth?

What if that means that I need to be ME? A genuine, authentic representation of the kind of man I actually *am*, rather than flogging myself in chasing an impossible goal, and neglecting to really know my children and partner in the meantime.

I admit I still have not found the perfect balance between work and family life, but I am making the right steps to try to do so.

I admit at times that I do struggle to always be the empathic father that I strive to be, yet again, I try.

I often fail to meet with old friends to catch up as much as I would love to, but I'm working on building in time to do so.

I acknowledge that it is hard for me to be able to go out on a proper 'date' with my wife and spend time as a couple because we have two young children. But I know that at this young age, they need our presence and we need theirs. This time will not last forever, and we can never get it back.

I might not be a hero, but I am no loser either. I admit I am less than cool at times, but I am not totally clueless with domestic life either.

I am human.

Whatever I am, I am trying to be the best father that I can be for our children, and be a loving, supportive partner to my wife.

I am none of the traditional labels of fatherhood, and I am all of them.

I am an Empathic Father.

Cheers,
Torsten

FIND OUT MORE

If you found this book useful and enjoyed its message, please consider leaving a review on your platform of choice (such as Amazon or Goodreads). It would really help spread the word about the importance of conscious, attached fatherhood, and let new dads out there know there are those of us sharing their situation.

REFERENCES & FURTHER READING

- Anthony DeBenedet, and Lawrence J. Cohen, *The Art of Roughhousing,* Quirk Books, 2011
- Alfie Kohn, *Unconditional Parenting*, Atria Books, 2005
- Diana and Michael Richardson, *Tantric Sex for Men*, Destiny Books, 2010
- Diana Richardson, *Tantric Orgasm for Women*, Destiny Books, 2004
- Dr Sue Johnson, *Hold Me Tight: Your Guide to the Most Successful Approach to Building Loving Relationships,* Piatkus, 2011
- Elizabeth Pantley, *The No-Cry Sleep Solution: Gentle Ways to Help Your Baby Sleep Through the Night*, McGraw-Hill Contemporary, 2002
- Lawrence J Cohen: *Playful Parenting*, Ballantine Books repl. 2012
- Meryn Callander: *Why Dads Leave: Insights and Resources for When Partners Become Parents*, Akasha Publications, 2012
- Oliver James, *Love Bombing: Reset Your Child's Emotional Thermostat,* Karnac Books, 2012
- Patrick M Houser: *Fathers-to-be-Handbook*, Creative Life Systems Ltd, 2007
- Sue Gerhardt: *Why Love Matters*, Routledge 2004
- Tom Hodgkinson: *The Idle Parent*, Penguin Books, 2009/2010
- William and Martha Sears: *The Attachment Parenting Book,* Little, Brown and Company, 2001

- Adele Faber & Elaine Mazlish: *Siblings Without Rivalry*, Piccadilly Press, 1999
- Steven R. Covey: The 7 Habits of Highly Effective People, Simon & Schuster Ltd., 2004
- Co-Sleeping References
    - The Family Bed by JL Morse
      http://jlmorse.com/titles/the-family-bed/
      This #1 Amazon Parenting Bestseller features safe cosleeping guidelines
    - Sarah Ockwell-Smith, *The Gentle Sleep Book: For Calm Babies, Toddlers And Pre-Schoolers*, Piatkus, 2015
    - Elizabeth Pantley's No Cry Sleep Solution
      http://www.pantley.com/elizabeth/books/0071381392.php?nid=169

WEBSITES REFERENCED AND/OR RECOMMENDED

- www.dadstalkcommunity.org
- www.parentsaslovers.com
- www.FathersToBe.org
- www.fathernation.com
- www.naturalpapa.com
- www.goodmenproject.com
- www.homebirth.org.uk
- www.familiality.co.uk
- www.attachmentparenting.org
- www.empoweredpapa.com
- www.mamaot.net
    - http://mamaot.com/2012/11/25/why-kids-should-play-with-baby-dolls-yes-even-boys/
- www.ladsandadsclub.com
- http://www.lotusbirth.net
- John Bowlby –Theory of Attachment
  http://www.simplypsychology.org/bowlby.html
- Hypnobirthing 'Effective home preparation' CD –
  www.natalhypnotherapy.co.uk
- Gerhard Pretorius http://www.familiality.co.uk/blog/?p=286

- John Gottman Couples Therapy - http://www.gottman.com/about-gottman-method-couples-therapy/
- Non-Violent Communication, Marshall **Rosenberg** https://www.youtube.com/watch?v=-dpk5Z7GIFs&list=PL16F02595B1BB9FA8
- Stephen R Covey http://article.wn.com/view/2014/07/25/Seek_First_to_Understand_/
- Dealing with Depression / PND in Men
    - http://raisingchildren.net.au/articles/men_and_postnatal_depression.html
    - http://www.bbc.co.uk/news/health-13454471
    - http://www.theguardian.com/society/2010/sep/08/postnatal-depression-fathers-men
    - http://www.mind.org.uk/information-support/types-of-mental-health-problems/anger/useful-contacts/#.VQw-n-ERRGl
    - http://www.nhs.uk/conditions/stress-anxiety-depression/pages/controlling-anger.aspx

ABOUT THE AUTHOR

 Torsten Klaus is a father to two boys and one girl, and is a Parenting Coach and Author. He has been working with children and families for more than a decade.

The founder of www.dadstalkcommunity.org, Torsten runs successful online and in person support groups for Dads and Grandads. He also teaches Developmental Baby Massage in his local community. He loves storytelling and is currently working on his second book for children.

Torsten lives with his family in the south-west of England, and stayed at home to care for his children between 2012 and 2014. He also runs Couples Counselling workshops, alongside his wife, Nedua at www.parentsaslovers.com

www.dadstalkcommunity.org
www.facebook.com/DadsTalk
Twitter: @EmpathicFathers
Email: onetreefamilyotf@gmail.com

OTHER TITLES BY TORSTEN KLAUS

MOSANDA AND THE SNOWMAN

A winter tale written and read by Torsten Klaus, this delightful audiobook is available from Ejunkie, Amazon and One Tree Family, and is suitable for all ages.

"Mosanda is a little girl who lives in a country on Africa's east coast. It's winter time and Mosanda sees lots of winter pictures in her books. She is fascinated by a cold frosty creature: a snowman. Mosanda decides that she wants to build her very own snowman. Will that be possible? Follow Mosanda on her extraordinary journey."

Mosanda and The Snowman. An audio story for children (4 years+). MP3, 23 minutes

A Tale Written & Read by Torsten Klaus

ABOUT THE PUBLISHERS: ONE TREE FAMILY

One Tree Family is an Independent Publisher dedicated to promoting original voices and the words they create.

www.onetreefamily.com
@OneTreeFamily on Twitter

We welcome submissions from aspiring authors and their digital pens, with particular interest in the following areas:

- Natural Living (Health, Parenting, Beauty)
- Homeschooling through Unschooling and everything in-between
- Attachment or Conscious Parenting
- Babywearing, Slings and Co-Sleeping
- Vegetarian, Vegan, Raw Foodism etc

Fiction or Non-Fiction, but make the words your own and we'll help the world read them.

Remember to check out our blog at
www.onetreefamily/otf-blog

unschadlipeurope.org

27875 571 067

korstenklaus @ pmx . net